The National Interest
and the Law of the Sea

COUNCIL *on*
FOREIGN
RELATIONS

Council Special Report No. 46
May 2009

Scott G. Borgerson

The National Interest
and the Law of the Sea

Mixed Sources
Product group from well-managed forests and other controlled sources
www.fsc.org Cert no. SW-COC-001530
© 1996 Forest Stewardship Council

FSC

Contents

Foreword

The oceans have long been a critical arena for international relations. Before there was air travel and instantaneous communication, people, goods, and ideas traveled the world by ship. For centuries a strong maritime presence—both military and commercial—has been essential for states with great power aspirations. Today, even with advances in technology, seaborne commerce remains the linchpin of the global economy. As the International Maritime Organization reports, "more than 90 percent of global trade is carried by sea." And beyond trade, a host of other issues, ranging from climate change and energy to defense and piracy, ensure that the oceans will hold considerable strategic interest well into the future.

In this Council Special Report, Scott G. Borgerson explores an important element of the maritime policy regime: the United Nations Convention on the Law of the Sea. He examines the international negotiations that led to the convention, as well as the history of debates in the United States over whether to join it. He then analyzes the strategic importance of the oceans for U.S. foreign policy today. The report ultimately makes a strong case for the United States to accede to the Convention on the Law of the Sea, contending that doing so would benefit U.S. national security as well as America's economic and environmental interests. Among other things, the report argues, accession to the convention would secure rights for U.S. commercial and naval ships, boost the competitiveness of American firms in activities at sea, and increase U.S. influence in important policy decisions, such as adjudications of national claims to potentially resource-rich sections of the continental shelf.

The National Interest and the Law of the Sea offers a combination of historical, legal, and strategic analysis. It illustrates how much of what the United States seeks to do in the world—be it deploying military forces abroad or ensuring adequate supplies of energy—depends in large measure on the sea. The result is an important contribution on a set of issues that has been central to national power and foreign policy for centuries.

Richard N. Haass
President
Council on Foreign Relations
May 2009

Acknowledgments

I am deeply grateful to the following people for helping me produce this report: John Temple Swing, Caitlyn Antrim, and Matthew Tinning of the Ocean Conservancy. They made significant and substantive contributions. Brian Donegan also deserves special mention for crafting whole sections and helping in all facets of the report's composition. His name deserves to be on the cover as much as mine. Of course, I alone accept full responsibility for this document and any shortcomings or omissions.

I am also indebted to Ambassador Thomas R. Pickering, who chaired the advisory committee. He and the committee provided invaluable wisdom throughout the drafting process. This report also benefited immeasurably from the help of the following CFR staff: Patricia Dorff and Lia Norton in Publications, Kaysie Brown in the International Institutions and Global Governance program, Sasha Polakow-Suransky in *Foreign Affairs*, and Melanie Gervacio Lin and my research associate Erika Wool in the Studies Program.

This publication and my fellowship were made possible by the generous support of the Robina Foundation and the International Institutions and Global Governance program. I am especially grateful to the program's director, Stewart M. Patrick, for his support. I am honored to in some small way be part of the program's important work.

Scott G. Borgerson

Council Special Report

Introduction

The 1982 Convention on the Law of the Sea—the instrument that created the overarching governance framework for nearly three-quarters of the earth's surface and what lies above and beneath it—has been signed and ratified by 156 countries and the European Community, but not by the United States. The Law of the Sea Convention, with annexes (hereafter in this report referred to as the "convention"), and the 1994 agreement on its implementation have been in force for more than a decade, but while the United States treats most parts of the convention as customary international law, it remains among only a handful of countries—and one of an even smaller number with coastlines, including Syria, North Korea, and Iran—to have signed but not yet acceded to the treaty.[1]

President Bill Clinton submitted the Law of the Sea Convention to the Senate for its approval in 1994, but despite numerous congressional hearings and even though the Senate Foreign Relations Committee (SFRC) twice recommended that the Senate give its consent,[2] the convention has yet to make it to the Senate floor.[3] The convention actually enjoys broad bipartisan support in Congress; has been endorsed by both the Clinton and George W. Bush administrations; is championed by the Joints Chiefs of Staff; and has been recommended by a wide array of interest groups in the United States, including the foremost national security, commercial, and environmental organizations.[4] Still, largely because of the threat of a filibuster from a vocal opposition, the convention has yet to receive a full Senate vote.

With last November's elections, the convention is once more in the news. The political balance of power has shifted in Washington, making the prospects of Senate approval likely. President Barack Obama, both during his tenure in the Senate and while on the campaign trail, expressed enthusiastic support for the convention. Vice President Joseph R. Biden Jr. was chairman of the SFRC when the convention was last recommended for approval in 2007, and Senator John Kerry (D-MA), the new chairman, strongly supports it, as does Senator Richard G. Lugar (R-IN), the committee's ranking Republican. During her confirmation hearings, Secretary of State Hillary Clinton stressed that getting the convention through the Senate would be a top priority for her State Department. And in February 2009, with Alaska governor Sarah Palin's backing, the National Governors Association came out strongly in support of the United States joining the treaty.

The convention is also getting a close look as a result of recent events, perhaps the most dramatic being a serious confrontation in March 2009 between U.S. and Chinese naval ships and Somali pirates taking a U.S. ship captain hostage in April. Piracy is growing exponentially off Somalia's coast and is threatening strategic shipping lanes. The polar ice cap, melting fast and on pace to be seasonally ice free by 2013, is drawing attention as well; the relatively pristine Arctic Ocean is becoming open to fishing, international shipping, and the development of an estimated 22 percent of the world's remaining undiscovered but technically recoverable hydrocarbon reserves.[5] There is a growing list of other emerging security, economic, and environmental maritime issues with important strategic implications for U.S. foreign policy, such as the rise of new naval powers like China and India, the delineation of vast amounts of ocean space on the outer continental shelf (OCS), and new commercial opportunities like deep-seabed mining. All of this is causing Washington to reconsider and reexamine the convention.

In many ways, the arguments surrounding the treaty are emblematic of the broader debate about the role of U.S. diplomacy in the post-9/11 world. Skeptics of the convention believe it is not needed, given the hegemonic strength of the U.S. Navy. And, they ask, why does the United States need to join this international agreement if it has gotten along fine so far without it? They also worry that the United States will undermine its sovereignty by incurring additional treaty obligations to international bodies established within the United Nations' system. In a fast-changing world, with new threats confronting the United States all the time, this camp holds that the United States needs to be able to respond as nimbly as possible, unencumbered by lengthy legal conventions that might restrict its freedom of action.

Supporters of the convention counter that the principles embodied in the treaty are the cornerstone of U.S. naval strategy and create the rule of law for prosecuting pirates and the growing number of other

threatening nonstate actors. They argue that the convention is important for economic reasons as well, as it creates legal certainty for all kinds
of commercial ocean uses, from offshore oil and gas to undersea cables
to deep-seabed mining, that favor U.S. interests. They also argue, from
an ecological perspective, that the convention helps the United States
assume a leadership position for dealing with collapsing fishing stocks,
pollution from land-based sources and ships, and the growing danger of
ocean waste. Convention advocates highlight how oceans are, by their
very nature, international and thus require a regime of international law
and collaborative approaches to their management. They point to the
1995 UN Fish Stocks Agreement as a prime example of how a carefully
constructed international accord negotiated within the framework of
the convention can provide for a legally binding conservation regime.
Recognizing the utility of this specific fisheries management tool, the
United States rapidly ratified this additional instrument as soon as it
was possible to do so in 1996. Lastly, supporters ask that if the United
States is not willing to accede to a convention that it requested, fundamentally shaped, and subsequently caused to be modified in order to
address its own concerns, then why in a multipolar world should other
countries follow its diplomatic leadership? In such a context, how will
expressions of U.S. commitments to the rule of law abroad be heard?

This report will fully examine both sides of the accession debate: the
wisdom of maintaining current U.S. policy of relying on large parts of
the convention as customary international law versus now officially
joining the 1982 Convention on the Law of the Sea. It will outline the
costs and benefits that would come from the Senate giving its consent
to the convention. It will examine all the foreign policy dimensions of
joining or not joining the convention, which are further elaborated in
greater legal detail in Appendix I, and the strategic imperative of one
course of action over another.

Given the extraordinary scope of the convention and the possibility of U.S. accession early in the Obama administration, this report is
intended to give a fresh appraisal of this complex and lengthy international agreement in light of the current geopolitical seascape, and to
weigh whether it is in U.S. strategic interests to finally join.

Background and Context

The 1982 Convention on the Law of the Sea is not a new construct; rather, it is the product of centuries of practice, three UN conferences (1958, 1960, and 1973–1982), and a subsequent agreement on implementation, negotiated from 1990 to 1994. Nor is the convention a new issue for the U.S. Senate. In force since 1994, the convention has been awaiting review since its transmission to the Senate by President Clinton in 1994. For a decade and a half the convention has been pending Senate approval and has been the subject of debate between a broad bipartisan constituency actively working toward accession and a vocal minority blocking legislative action in the belief that it would burden the United States with additional international commitments. Before examining these viewpoints in light of U.S. strategic interests today, it is useful to understand the principal tenets of the convention and its historical context.

BRIEF HISTORY OF THE LAW OF THE SEA, FROM HUGO GROTIUS TO TODAY

Creating an international ocean governance framework has its roots in sixteenth-century European imperialism. As states increasingly competed for trade routes and territory, two theories of ocean use collided head-on. On one side, Spain and Portugal claimed national ownership of vast areas of ocean space, including the Gulf of Mexico and the entire Atlantic Ocean, which the Catholic Church declared should be divided between them. Opposed to this were the proponents of "freedom of the seas," a theory of vital concern to the great trading firms like the Dutch East India Company. Since no nation could really enforce claims to such enormous areas, and given the need of all the rising colonial powers to have assured access to their overseas territories, it is not surprising that the proponents of freedom of the seas, the foremost of whom was the Dutch jurist Hugo Grotius, emerged triumphant. That concept became the basis of modern ocean law.

Over the next three centuries, the concept of freedom of the seas became almost universally accepted, subject only to the exception that in an area extending three miles from the shoreline, or roughly the range of iron cannons of the day, the coastal state was sovereign. Its control, however, was not absolute. Vessels of other countries were given the right of passage through the territorial sea so long as such passage was "innocent"—that is to say, "not prejudicial to the peace, good order or security of the coastal state."[6] The nineteenth century witnessed a steady increase in ocean commerce, and freedom of the seas came to be qualified by the concept of "reasonable" use—basically, respect for the rights of others.

It was during the twentieth century, with its discoveries of important resources, such as oil, and a sharp rise in ocean uses generally, that the accepted principles began to erode. Customary law, dependent on slow, incremental growth, could no longer move fast enough to provide generally acceptable solutions to new problems. Traditional uses multiplied. Both the world fish catch and the gross tonnage of merchant ships quadrupled in the twenty-five years from 1950 to 1975. However, the real spur to the seaward expansion of territorial claims had come a decade earlier with the discovery of oil under the continental shelf off the coast of the United States. That led President Harry S. Truman in 1945 to proclaim that henceforth the United States had the exclusive right to explore and exploit the mineral resources of its continental shelf beyond the traditional three-mile limit.[7]

As frequently happens in international affairs, this action sparked reaction. The Truman Proclamation was soon followed by other unilateral declarations. Chile, Ecuador, and Peru, for example, countries with only narrow continental margins and thus little chance of finding oil, countered by declaring seaward extensions of their jurisdictions to two hundred miles—thereby encompassing fisheries for species, including tuna, that were important to distant-water fishermen from other countries, notably the United States. That set the stage for international conflict that continued into the mid-1970s in the form of the repeated seizure, particularly by Ecuador, of ships of the U.S. tuna fleet based in San Diego found within the declared two-hundred-mile limit but well outside the traditional three-mile territorial sea.

Unilateral extensions were also of growing concern to the world's major maritime powers, particularly the United States and the Soviet Union. As more and more coastal states started claiming territorial seas broader than three miles (in several cases, as much as twelve miles, but in some, particularly in Latin America, far beyond), the maritime nations feared that their freedom of navigation on, over, and under critical portions of the world's oceans might be severely curtailed. They were particularly concerned that they would lose their high-seas freedoms in the 116 straits, including those of Malacca, Dover, Gibraltar, and Hormuz, that, at their narrowest point, were more than six miles but less than twenty-four miles in width. If these 116 straits became territorial seas, the rules of innocent passage would require, for example, that submarines operate on the surface, not submerged, and that overflight by aircraft be prohibited without the prior consent of the coastal state.

The maritime nations did their best but failed to cap these extensions in two UN conferences—the first in 1958, and the second in 1960—the results of which were never widely accepted. By the mid-1960s, they were eager to try again, and they lent their weight to the growing calls for a new UN conference on the law of the sea. Their calls were not the only ones. Many developing nations in the Third World were concerned about preserving international rights to nonliving resources beyond the limits of national jurisdiction. In 1967, these concerns were crystallized in a remarkable speech before the General Assembly by Arvid Pardo, then the Maltese delegate. Pardo was viewed sympathetically throughout much of the world when he asked the UN to declare the seabed and the ocean floor "underlying the seas beyond the limits of present national jurisdiction" to be "the common heritage of mankind" and not subject to appropriation by any nation for its sole use. He urged the creation of a new kind of international agency that, acting as trustee for all countries, would assume jurisdiction over the seabed and supervise the development and recovery of its resources "for the benefit of all mankind," with the net proceeds to be used primarily to promote the development of the poorer countries of the world.[8]

Developing countries liked the idea for several reasons. First, since the value of the resources was then believed to be considerable, some thought it would lead to substantial development assistance for the poorest countries. Second, it gave developing countries a chance to become partners in, rather than subjects of, resource development. Developed countries also liked the prospect of a source of development funds that, for once, would not be a direct drain on their treasuries. The major maritime countries also saw the idea as the natural vehicle to finally provide a counterweight to the seaward expansion of coastal-state jurisdictions.

Whatever the motive, the concept of the common heritage was embodied in a "Declaration of Principles Governing the Sea-bed and Ocean Floor Beyond the Limits of National Jurisdiction,"[9] which was adopted by the General Assembly by a vote of 106–0, with the United States voting in favor and only the Soviet bloc abstaining. The declaration called for the establishment of a new regime to oversee management of this area and to ensure the equitable sharing of benefits, with specific reference to the needs of developing countries. A companion resolution called for the convening in 1973 of a comprehensive conference to cover all ocean issues on the international agenda.

The stage was now set for the Third United Nations Conference on the Law of the Sea, which formally convened in New York in December 1973. It was the largest international conference ever held, with virtually every country in the world represented, many of them relatively new and with no prior experience in dealing with ocean issues. There was even a subgroup to look after the interests of fifty-one landlocked or geographically disadvantaged states. In essence, the conference was charged with the formidable task of creating a comprehensive framework for managing ocean uses that would be acceptable to the international community.

What were U.S. objectives in the negotiations? On what can be considered the sovereignty front, preserving freedoms of navigation were paramount, but there were also a number of other objectives, such as threats to fisheries and marine mammal conservation; protection of the marine environment, in particular from the growing threat of vessel-source pollution; and the preservation of the high-seas freedom of scientific research. All of these, like freedoms of navigation, were being whittled away by claims of exclusive control accompanying the many extensions of coastal-state jurisdiction. To strengthen against these extensions, the convention sought the establishment of third-party settlement mechanisms for disputes, particularly those over boundaries that were already being exacerbated by new jurisdictional claims.

On what can be called the deep-seabed front, there was the effort to create a regime to manage resources beyond national jurisdictions. The primary U.S. objective was to help create a strong, viable organization that would be effective against the further-seaward claims of coastal states. At the same time, the United States wanted to ensure access to the deep seabed for U.S.-based companies on reasonable terms and conditions that would offer the prospect of a fair profit in the light of the technical difficulties to be surmounted and the large capital investments required for development.

How well did the United States fare during the nearly ten years of negotiations that followed? Most observers believe that, as a whole, the convention met U.S. objectives reasonably well, even though the Reagan administration, which came to power in 1981, concluded that defects of the design for a seabed regime would prevent President Ronald Reagan from signing the final convention. Certainly, on the sovereignty side, the final Convention on the Law of the Sea met every significant U.S. objective.

Most important of all, the breadth of the territorial sea was capped at twelve miles, while a new transit passage regime was created that, for all practical purposes, preserved freedom of navigation and overflight of the international straits. High-seas freedoms were also preserved in the three newly created jurisdictional zones beyond the twelve-mile territorial sea: the contiguous zone out to twenty-four miles, where a coastal state could enforce customs and immigration laws; the 188-mile exclusive economic zone (EEZ), which carried the coastal state's jurisdiction over living and nonliving resources out to a total of two hundred miles; and the new archipelagic zones, which otherwise would have become internal waters of archipelagic states such as Indonesia and the Philippines, placing significant restrictions on navigation freedoms previously enjoyed in these areas. The convention also established procedures for extending coastal-state jurisdiction over areas of continental shelf beyond two hundred miles.

On the environmental front, the United States scored several important victories. It got the conference to agree to international standards for vessel-source pollution. There would be only one set of standards, worldwide, with which all vessels would have to comply. At the same time, the conference agreed to maintain the traditional right of port states to enact and enforce standards higher than the international ones for vessels entering their harbors. That was important to the United States, since an estimated 90 percent of all shipping off U.S. coasts is on its way to or from American seaports.

LEGAL BOUNDARIES OF THE OCEANS AND AIRSPACE

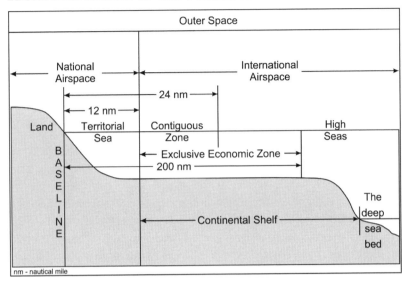

Source: *The Commander's Handbook on the Law of Naval Operations*, www.nwc.navy.mil/cnws/ild/documents/1-14M_(Jul_2007)_(NWP).pdf.

The Reagan administration thought that, by and large, the convention had gotten it right. Indeed, it later declared that the United States would voluntarily abide by all non-seabed parts of the convention.[10] The Reagan administration's objections were directed mainly at the deep-seabed side of the negotiations—the design of and the powers to be given to the new regime for governance of the mineral resource recovery in the area beyond national jurisdictions. The philosophical argument was that the United States should be able to go where it wanted and take what it wanted on a "first come, first served" basis. President Reagan would have preferred no regime at all governing the international seabed, but he realized that this was a fait accompli given the late stages of the negotiations. In the end, the Reagan administration declared it could accept Part XI only if certain changes were made in six areas having to do with matters like technology transfer, and if the United States preserved a de facto veto power in the governing organs of the new authority so that no financial obligations could be imposed on the United States without its consent. When these changes were not made by 1982, the Reagan administration refused to sign the convention.

All six of the Reagan administration's objections were fixed to the satisfaction of the United States in a subsequent supplemental agreement that was negotiated and signed by most states, including the United States, in 1994. By now, it has been adopted and ratified by most of the original signatories to the 1982 convention.

BRIEF HISTORY OF THE LAW OF THE SEA IN THE SENATE

On July 29, 1994, President Bill Clinton signed the Agreement on the Implementation of Part XI of the Convention on the Law of the Sea. He sent the agreement, along with the 1982 convention, to the Senate on October 7, 1994 (Appendix II). The following month, Republicans won control of the Senate, and in January 1995, Senator Jesse Helms (R-NC) became chairman of the Senate Foreign Relations Committee. Worried that the convention had not been fixed and that it sacrificed U.S. sovereignty, Senator Helms refused to hold committee hearings.

In 2003, Senator Richard Lugar succeeded Helms as chairman and, with the encouragement of the Bush administration, put the convention on the SFRC agenda. Senator Lugar held hearings, beginning with public witnesses and followed by government and industry witnesses a week later. In 2004, additional public hearings were held by the Armed Services Committee and the Committee on Environment and Public Works. A closed hearing was held by the Select Committee on Intelligence, which determined that joining the convention would not adversely affect U.S. intelligence activities. The SFRC prepared a draft resolution of advice and consent, and recommended Senate approval by a unanimous recommendation. The convention was sent to the full Senate, only to be delayed when then Senate majority leader William Frist (R-TN) did not bring it to the floor for a vote.

Senator Frist declined to run for reelection in 2006, and the Democrats won a majority in the midterm elections. With Senator Harry Reid (D-NV) as majority leader and Senator Joseph Biden (D-DE) taking over as chair of the SFRC, prospects for approval of the convention brightened. Letters of support from National Security Adviser Stephen Hadley and President Bush gave further impetus (see Appendix II).

However, Chairman Biden and the next ranking committee member, Senator Christopher Dodd (D-CT), were actively campaigning for the Democratic presidential nomination, and little progress was made during the early 2007 session of Congress. Eventually, testimony was taken during fall hearings, and the SFRC received letters from the chair and ranking member of the Armed Services Committee and the Select Committee on Intelligence, reaffirming their prior support of the convention. On October 31, 2007, the SFRC again approved the convention by a vote of 17–4, and the official report and recommendation for approval were submitted to the full Senate in December.

By the late autumn of 2007, the convention had become a small but notable issue in the Republican presidential campaign. Senator John McCain (R-AZ), who had a decadelong history of supporting the treaty, changed his position and opposed the convention. By early 2008, the heat of the presidential campaign brought progress on the convention to a halt. Then, following the election, the Senate's attention was taken by the growing economic crisis, precluding consideration of the convention during the lame-duck session.

Under Senate rules, treaties must be reconsidered by the SFRC in each new Congress. While the committee must begin the process again, it will be able to draw upon the extensive hearings held in 2003, 2004, and 2007 to inform its next review.

Oceans and National Interests

Oceans cover nearly three-quarters of the earth and have a profound significance to U.S. national security, yet they are often overlooked. Half the world's population lives within fifty miles of a coast (and 10 percent live within six miles). The oceans are marine highways, carrying 90 percent of U.S. imports and exports, and most of the world's oil passes through shipping choke points such as the Suez Canal and the Straits of Malacca. The oceans are a theater of conflict, a space in which traditional navies extend sovereign power, and a frontier where pirates, drug traffickers, and human smugglers proliferate. In peacetime, the ability of U.S. forces to navigate and overfly the oceans is a critical deterrent to conflict. The Law of the Sea Convention addresses all these issues and also includes articles covering traditional geostrategic concerns, such as naval mobility and maintaining what the early-twentieth-century American naval theorist Admiral Alfred Thayer Mahan called "sea lanes of communication," the lifelines of the U.S. economy. It is by way of the oceans that the United States is able to conduct international trade and project military power abroad.

From a maritime perspective, the United States is an island. Commercial shipping is what carries the world to America and America to the world. Reverberations from Iranian naval provocations in the Strait of Hormuz in 2008 and recent piracy in the Indian Ocean off Somalia's coast demonstrate just how critical it is to keep shipping lanes open. That is nothing new. The oceans have always figured prominently in American history, dating back to the earliest days when maritime links bound the colonies to the British Empire. Following independence, maritime issues were factors in almost every major diplomatic event, including the 1798–1800 quasi-war with France, which was essentially a naval contest; the beginnings of the U.S. Navy combatting Barbary pirates in the Mediterranean; and the *Chesapeake-Leopard* affair, which helped spark the War of 1812.

The list of other important maritime events in American history is a long one: for example, the repercussions of the North blockading the South during the Civil War; the sinking of the USS *Maine* on the eve of the Spanish-American War; the Great White Fleet announcing the United States as a world power; the maritime provisions of Woodrow Wilson's League of Nations and the naval treaties of the 1920s; the 1940 destroyers-for-bases agreement that sent fifty U.S. destroyers to Britain for use in World War II in exchange for land rights to British possessions; liberty ships, the now ubiquitous maritime containers (a U.S. invention); and undersea communication cables, to name but a few.[11] The oceans have been central to the American experience, whether as an arena for combat and struggle, as an avenue for the flow of commerce and people, as a source of fishing and resources, or as a wellspring of inspiration and challenge for Americans since the nation's beginning. The oceans have served both as a moat, shielding a rising power from foreign adversaries, and as a bridge, linking the United States to the wider world. The oceans undergird international relations and have been central to the making of U.S. foreign policy.

The oceans are vital to U.S. national interests for reasons beyond traditional national security. They shape the planet's weather and climate. Oceans redistribute heat from the tropics to cooler regions (e.g., western Europe), which profoundly affects the habitability of those lands. They serve as massive sinks for carbon dioxide (CO_2) emissions, thereby slowing global warming. However, they are in a dire environmental predicament because, since they absorb CO_2, they are rapidly becoming more acidic, making the marine environment less hospitable to the ecosystems that humankind depends upon. Dramatic human-caused increases in nutrient elements (nitrogen, phosphorous, iron, etc.) that enter the oceans via rivers and air currents; the physical alteration of coastal and marine ecosystems from development and seafloor-disturbing activities; and the introduction of alien marine species into new habitats all have profound effects on marine ecosystems that are crucial to U.S. national security interests.

And then there is fishing, the greatest threat to the oceans' ecosystem. From the early days of the cod fishery that supported New England and fed Europe to today's $14 billion industry, commercial fishing is important to the U.S. economy.[12] The oceans, however, have now been fished to dangerously low levels and are at a tipping point, beyond which many fish stocks might not rebound. In just the last half century, fish, which were previously thought of as an inexhaustible resource, have been reduced to alarmingly low levels. According to scientific studies, 90 percent of large predatory fish are now gone.[13] No fish stocks in the world have been left underdeveloped; nearly half have been fully exploited, about one-third have been overexploited, and about one-quarter are deemed to have "crashed."[14] More than a billion people depend on fish as their major source of protein, and a collapse in global fishing stocks would not only affect an important sector of the U.S. economy but also create conditions that would exacerbate existing political tensions in countries like Bangladesh, Indonesia, and the Philippines to the detriment of U.S. interests.

As a result of these threats to the oceans and marine species and ecosystems, the United States is being confronted by new maritime challenges. The ability to conduct marine scientific research throughout the oceans to better understand and respond to these challenges is crucial. The rapid degradation of the world's coral reefs, population explosions of jellyfish, and toxic phytoplankton blooms are signs of mismanagement that hint at unprecedented ocean environmental changes inimical to U.S. interests. For example, the Arctic's sea ice is melting rapidly and is opening this relatively pristine region to fishing, international shipping, and the development of nearly a quarter of the world's remaining undiscovered but technically recoverable hydrocarbon reserves.

The oceans should be thought of from an interdisciplinary perspective. They are more than a place of recreation; ocean issues include serious challenges for policymakers and real implications for U.S. national security. The oceans are vast, and the issues involved are so numerous that they do not fit neatly into any single official's inbox. There is no ocean czar, nor, for that matter, is any senior official on the National Security Council (NSC) charged with overseeing ocean issues solely (although there is an NSC maritime policy coordinating committee). Ocean issues fall under the purview of the departments of Defense, State, Commerce, Homeland Security, Transportation, and Treasury, among others, as well as under the Council on Environmental Quality, the Office of Science and Technology Policy, and the authority of numerous congressional committees. Important to all but owned by no one, oceans and the policies affecting them have been adrift without a senior champion with the president's ear. That is a profound weakness in U.S. governance, because ocean issues are critical to the country's national interests and central to U.S. foreign policy.

ARGUMENTS FOR AND AGAINST THE LAW OF THE SEA CONVENTION

Discussions of the convention should take into account the oceans' historic importance to U.S. national interests as well as maritime challenges facing the country today. Whether the convention expands the rule of law or sacrifices sovereignty is the question at the heart of the accession debate.

Opponents of the convention argue that there is no need to join the treaty because, with the world's hegemonic navy, the United States can treat the parts of the convention it likes as customary international law, following the convention's guidelines when it suits American interests and pursuing a unilateral course of action when it does not. They also argue that the convention is an unforgivable forfeiture of U.S. sovereignty to states that mean American interests harm. Supporters counter by saying that the convention expands the rule of law over the vast expanse of the world's oceans and contains provisions that could actually extend U.S. sovereignty. They also believe that shunning the convention is a tone-deaf response to the spirit of multilateralism and that, beyond undermining specific ocean policy issues and freezing the United States out of the convention's decision-making bodies, it tarnishes America's diplomatic reputation at a critical moment in international relations.

Debating the wisdom of whether to enter into international agreements is as old as the nation itself. Stung by the controversy over the 1794 Jay Treaty and the emergence of bitter partisanship between anglophile Federalists and francophile Democratic-Republicans (who felt the United States betrayed its French midwife when negotiating with the British in light of the 1778 treaties of Amity and Commerce), George Washington warned in his 1796 farewell address against "permanent alliances." In the centuries that followed, two distinct camps emerged in the American foreign policy tradition: one was isolationist, seeking to hide behind the Monroe Doctrine and remain aloof from corrupt, European deal-making; the other was more internationalist, seeking a more active United States in world affairs.[15] Debates for and against the convention roughly fit within these two categories.

Proponents of the convention, who can be assumed to include almost all Democrats and moderate Republicans (by most accounts, a large enough bloc to achieve a two-thirds majority, as required by the

Constitution for the United States to join the convention), have been frustrated to date by a passionate minority that strongly believes it is not in U.S. interests to join the convention. Opponents of the treaty argue that the convention unnecessarily commits the United States to follow rules designed by states hoping to constrain American freedom of action. Their specific objections to the convention are crystallized in the minority views submitted for the record the last time the convention was favorably voted out of the SFRC in December 2007: "[C]ertain provisions of the [convention], particularly those dealing with navigation, have merit," but overall and especially in regard to the dispute resolution, "[i]t is puzzling why we would want to submit to a judicial authority selected by the United Nations, given the organization's corruption scandals, and the fact that of the 152 countries Party to the treaty, the median voting coincidence with the United States in the General Assembly was less than 20 percent. This treaty subjects the United States to a governing body that is hostile to American interests."[16] Other provisions found objectionable included "taxes" assessed to outer continental shelf activities; fear of judicial activism by the Law of the Sea Tribunal, especially with regard to articles relating to land-based sources of pollution that are called a "backdoor Kyoto Protocol"; and a belief the convention will severely curtail U.S. intelligence-gathering activities.

On an item-by-item assessment, however, these arguments are found to be lacking (Appendix I in far greater detail addresses the convention's opponents' critical concerns). With regard to dispute settlement, the United States has indicated that it would choose arbitration as stated in the draft resolution of advice and consent; it cannot be forced into any other dispute settlement mechanism. Specifically, Article 287 of the convention reads: "[I]f the parties to a dispute have not accepted the same procedure for the settlement of the dispute, it may be submitted only to arbitration in accordance with Annex VII, unless the parties otherwise agree." Under no circumstances can the United States be subjected to any dispute resolution procedures without its consent. Also, the convention does not assess a "tax" but, rather, includes modest revenue-sharing provisions from exploitation of oil and gas from the seabed beyond the EEZ that have been supported by every president since Richard Nixon, including Ronald Reagan. These resources were far outside any earlier claim made by the United States, and the agreement to the modest payments was part of a package deal that included willingness to recognize extension of U.S. control over the resources on the continental margin beyond two hundred nautical miles, which may encompass well over a million square kilometers of potentially exploitable minerals. That the payments are, indeed, modest is attested to by the support of the U.S. oil and gas industry for these convention provisions. With regard to a "backdoor Kyoto Protocol," Bush administration officials testified before the SFRC that the convention does not apply the Kyoto Protocol to the United States, either directly or indirectly. The convention's provisions include no cause for legal action regarding land-based sources of pollution; they only represent agreement that states are responsible for addressing pollution under their own laws and enforcement. Lastly, the heads of the U.S. Navy and intelligence agencies have testified before the Senate Intelligence Committee that the convention does not impede intelligence-gathering activities; on the contrary, the rights afforded to the United States by the convention significantly empower U.S. intelligence-gathering abilities.

On balance, the arguments in favor of the convention far outweigh those opposed, which is the reason the convention has attracted such a diverse and bipartisan constituency. As presidents Clinton and George W. Bush forcefully argued in their written communications with the Senate (Appendix II), objections to the 1982 convention were substantively addressed in the 1994 agreement on implementation. Continuing to treat most parts of the convention as customary international law, as the United States does now, literally leaves it without a seat at the table in important decision-making bodies established by the convention, such as the Commission on the Limits of the Continental Shelf (CLCS); weakens the hand the United States can play in negotiations over critical maritime issues, such as rights in the opening of the Arctic Ocean; and directly undercuts U.S. ability to respond to emerging challenges, such as increasing piracy in the Indian Ocean. Joining or not joining the convention is more than an academic debate. There are tangible costs that grow by the day if the United States remains outside the convention.

The majority view of the SFRC and the opinion of every major ocean constituency group is that joining the convention is in America's foreign policy interests. Debating the merits of internationalism versus unilateralism is a great U.S. tradition, but the irony is that the convention actually allows for an expansion of U.S. sovereignty: freedom of movement for a powerful navy; a legal tool for U.S. forces to combat scourges at sea, such as piracy, drug trafficking, and human smuggling; and a process for extending U.S. jurisdiction over a vast amount of ocean space equal to half the size of the Louisiana Purchase.

As the next section of this report details, acceding to the convention would advance a long list of national security, economic, and environmental issues of strategic importance to the United States. Beyond establishing the rules for territorial seas and exclusive economic zones, the convention establishes regimes for managing shipping fleets, fish, and pollutants that do not abide by national boundaries. The Law of the Sea Convention includes specific provisions guaranteeing freedom of navigation for merchant fleets and navies, and sets firm limits on jurisdiction to prevent "creeping sovereignty" by a few aggressive coastal states eager to unilaterally extend their authority seaward. The convention is used to prosecute pirates and is the basis for the Proliferation Security Initiative (PSI) to interdict weapons of mass destruction (WMD).

In addition to these traditional geostrategic issues, the convention is also germane to a host of other ocean uses, some traditional and others new. It governs commercial activities on, in, and under the world's oceans. With one-third of the world's oil and gas already produced offshore, this is especially important, as the future of hydrocarbon extraction is in ever-deeper waters. The convention establishes the jurisdictional framework for rules governing this industry operating on the extended continental shelf. Deep-seabed mining is also an emerging industry, and the convention establishes, together with the 1994 agreement on implementation, the legal regime for extracting resources from the ocean floor. The International Seabed Authority (ISA), created by the convention, introduces chambered voting, a permanent seat for the United States in the executive decision-making bodies, and the power to block adoption of rules and budgets that are counter to U.S. interests. The convention is also crucial for helping to manage commercial uses yet to be envisioned. Innovation and new technologies have played an essential role in sustaining U.S. prosperity and preeminence, and American entrepreneurs will undoubtedly discover future opportunities in the oceans.

The convention as a whole reflects traditional U.S. interests. It has been supported by both Republican and Democratic administrations and enjoys the endorsement of major maritime organizations. Should the United States join the Law of the Sea Convention? What has changed to make accession so urgent? As the next section chronicles, a growing list of pressing maritime issues of strategic importance covered by the convention makes prompt accession to the treaty a U.S. national interest.

Strategic Imperatives

Immediate U.S. accession to the treaty is imperative to advance critical U.S. national interests. These stakes can be grouped into three general "baskets": national security, economic, and environmental. Each day the convention is in force—and each day its various organs make ocean policy and set legal precedent—the United States is in effect marginalizing itself. It is also placing itself at a disadvantage by being unable to mobilize the convention to advance its interests through new initiatives or by means of the credibility that accompanies being a state party. The following paragraphs summarize the abiding U.S. interests in becoming party to the Law of the Sea Convention.

NATIONAL SECURITY

To date, U.S. military forces have successfully protected American shipping and the homeland from sea-based attack without the benefits of the convention. Why is it imperative to join the convention now? What does the convention provide that distinguishes it from existing treaties and the customary international law upon which the United States has depended for the past five decades?

In short, the convention provides the protection of binding international law in four categories of essential navigation and overflight rights. Together, these rights ensure the strategic and operational mobility of U.S. military forces and the free flow of international commerce at sea. Joining the convention guarantees that 156 states recognize the following basic rights of U.S. military forces, commercial ships, civilian aircraft, and the foreign-flagged vessels that carry commerce vital to U.S. economic security:

- *Right of Innocent Passage.* The surface transit of any ship or submarine through the territorial seas of foreign nations without prior notification or permission.
- *Right of Transit Passage.* The unimpeded transit of ships, aircraft, and submerged submarines in their normal modes through and over straits used for international navigation, and the approaches to those straits.
- *Right of Archipelagic Sealanes Passage.* The unimpeded transit of ships, aircraft, and submerged submarines in their normal modes through and over all normal passage routes used for international navigation of "archipelagic waters," such as those claimed by the Philippines and Indonesia.
- *Freedom of the High Seas.* The freedoms of navigation, overflight, and use of the seabed for laying undersea cables or pipes on the high seas and within the exclusive economic zone of a coastal state.

Further, the convention secures additional important rights for warships, including U.S. Coast Guard cutters, and government-operated noncommercial ships, such as those operated by the Military Sealift Command:

- *Right of Visit.* Warships may visit and board vessels reasonably suspected of being stateless or engaged in piracy. That right is critically important to ensure the legitimacy of many maritime security operations, including U.S. counternarcotic and antiproliferation operations, such as the Proliferation Security Initiative.
- *Right of Sovereign Immunity.* Warships and government-operated noncommercial ships enjoy complete immunity from the jurisdiction of any state other than the flag state.

The convention also provides the first concrete definitions—U.S.-preferred definitions—of a coastal state's territorial sea, contiguous zone, and jurisdiction in the increasingly important and often contentious exclusive economic zone. The United States has previously asserted these rights and employed these definitions by relying on the protections of customary international law and the provisions of the

1958 Geneva Conventions. What makes these protections so vital to U.S. national security? Why now? What has happened to make joining the convention a national security imperative?

The world has changed dramatically in the last half century, making the legal tools and protections the convention provides essential for the United States to shape and influence the security environment of the twenty-first century. The political polarization of the Cold War has yielded to a rise of both nations and nationalism. In 1958, there were eighty-two members of the United Nations; today there are 192. The North Atlantic Treaty Organization, the Americas' bedrock national security alliance, has grown from fifteen member nations to twenty-six members and twenty-four partners. While the threat of international conventional and nuclear war has diminished, the transnational threats of WMD proliferation and violent extremism by nonstate interests with international reach have mushroomed. Expanding populations, combined with the growth of the newly industrialized economies, have fueled an increasing demand for and competition over natural resources. The energy security of the United States and every major world economy now depends on a global fuel market in which half of the world's oil travels by sea, with most passing through a handful of strategic straits. Global commerce is the cornerstone of every nation's economic security, with approximately 90 percent of both international physical and electronic trade traveling across the sea in ships or under the sea in cables.[17]

Changes in politics and economics have been matched or exceeded by changes in the physical world. Readily exploited reserves of oil and gas have been depleted. Entire species of highly valued apex predators, like tuna, and less palatable but economically critical forage fish, like menhaden, are collapsing. Meanwhile, a warming climate is opening the Arctic Ocean to navigation, providing access to previously unreachable resources and bringing about competing jurisdictional claims over this frontier.

In 2008, the National Defense Strategy signed by Secretary of Defense Robert M. Gates reinforced the main tenets of the Cooperative Strategy for 21st Century Seapower, issued in 2007 by the chief of naval operations and the commandants of the Marine Corps and the Coast Guard.[18] Both strategies emphasize that the prevention of war is the best way to achieve U.S. national security, and both highlight the fact that a strengthened system of alliances and partnerships is an essential component of building stability, collective security, and trust. The Cooperative Strategy for 21st Century Seapower is aptly named and uniquely relevant when considering the question of whether to join the convention. Its main points are:

– Preventing wars is as important as winning wars.
– U.S. maritime power comprises six core capabilities that emphasize preventing war and building partnerships: deterrence, sea control, power projection, maritime security, humanitarian assistance, and disaster response.
– Expanded cooperative relationships with other nations will contribute to the security and stability of the maritime domain to the benefit of all.
– Trust and confidence cannot be surged; they must be built over time while mutual understanding and respect are promoted.
– Global maritime partnerships provide a cooperative approach to maritime security, promoting the rule of law by countering piracy, terrorism, weapons proliferation, drug trafficking, and other illicit activities.

This strategy predicts that "increased competition for resources, coupled with scarcity, may encourage nations to exert wider claims of sovereignty over greater expanses of ocean, waterways, and natural resources—potentially resulting in conflict."

Why are the provisions and protections of the convention vital to implementing U.S. national defense and maritime strategies? Why now? All six core capabilities of U.S. maritime forces are predicated upon legally certain freedom of navigation and overflight, as defined by the United States and codified in the convention. Joining the convention supports the strategic and operational mobility of American air, surface, and submarine forces. It provides legal guarantees for those forces to transit the high seas, exclusive economic zones, international straits, and archipelagic sea routes during times of crisis. It supports the freedom of those forces to legally conduct military survey, reconnaissance, and intelligence gathering under the terms and conditions the United States prefers. It allows the high-seas interdiction of stateless vessels and illegal activities under frameworks such as the Proliferation Security Initiative, using the protocols the United States carefully crafted to conform to the convention. Most recently, this year articles 100 and 105 of the convention have been applied as the basis of an agreement with Kenya to prosecute Somali pirates apprehended in the Indian Ocean.

Implementing the maritime and national security strategies in the current geopolitical environment requires that U.S. armed forces be provided not only with the convention's rights, freedoms, and protections necessary to facilitate military operations but also with the legal legitimacy necessary to build partnerships, trust, and confidence with nations around the globe. Currently, American armed forces are hamstrung when the United States publicly solicits other nations to join it in enforcing the rule of law, while at the same time refuses to join the international legal frameworks necessary to establish such rule. The U.S. failure to join the convention has directly prevented expansion of the PSI with some critically important Pacific countries. Although these countries are supportive of U.S. counterproliferation efforts, they indicate that U.S. refusal to join the convention has eroded their confidence that the United States will abide by international law when conducting PSI interdiction activities. Remaining outside the convention risks further damaging American efforts to develop cooperative maritime partnerships, such as PSI, and undermining implementation of U.S. security strategies that require the confidence and trust of other nations.

Joining the convention would provide the United States with the opportunity to take a leadership role in the first truly global maritime partnership—a coalition of 156 nations committed to freedom of navigation, the free flow of global commerce, the protection of legitimate sovereignty, the suppression of illegal use of the sea, and the peaceful resolution of maritime disputes.

Joining the convention would also provide important diplomatic tools for those times when the United States must act swiftly and alone to exercise its right of self-defense. In such situations, the leaders of states party to the convention may lack the skill or the will to positively influence their domestic constituencies that oppose U.S. actions. The convention not only guarantees nearly universally recognized legal protection for the movement of U.S. military forces, it also provides vital political protection for foreign leaders who must resist domestic challenges to U.S. use of airspace and water space within their jurisdiction.

That protection may prevent short-lived but necessary unilateral action by the United States from damaging long-nurtured international relationships.

In short, the convention is vital to carrying out the president's national security strategy, including serving as the underpinnings supporting U.S. force projection abroad and the legal armor for safeguarding America at home.

ECONOMIC

The convention provides the legal framework for commercial uses of the sea. It establishes clear lines of jurisdiction for states to govern economic activity within their territorial seas and exclusive economic zones. (For example, whether the United States should lift offshore drilling prohibitions is and will remain purely an internal issue.) The convention addresses not only hydrocarbon exploration and extraction but establishes a government's framework for all commercial uses, such as renewable energy projects like wind, current and tidal power, commercial fishing, and aquaculture. The convention also establishes a legal framework for international uses of the sea that extend across national jurisdictions. It guarantees the freedom of navigation for commercial ships and aircraft while providing for the prompt release of U.S. flagged vessels seized by foreign states. The convention also facilitates the laying of submarine cables, the information backbone of the world economy. And it provides the basic rules for conserving and managing transboundary fish stocks, further elaborated in the 1995 UN Fish Stocks Agreement. While all these economic issues are vitally important, there are two that specifically create a sense of urgency for the United States to accede to the Law of the Sea Convention.

The first is benefiting from the rules relating to extending national jurisdiction over the extended continental shelf. Article 76 of the convention automatically gives states exclusive economic rights out to two hundred nautical miles from their shores (determined from a carefully defined "baseline"). In addition, they can also assert sovereign rights over natural resources in the extended continental shelf beyond two hundred nautical miles if the shelf extension meets certain criteria as outlined in the convention. The convention creates a procedure to facilitate the process of a coastal state submitting claims over its outer continental shelf. The office managing this procedure, the Commission on the Limits of the Continental Shelf, consists of twenty-one technical experts who review a country's claims to ensure that the bathymetric and geological evidence submitted meets the convention's criteria. It is an orderly process, and the following states, in chronological order, have made submissions, some of them already approved by the CLCS: the Russian Federation, Brazil, Australia, Ireland, New Zealand, Norway, Mexico, Barbados, the UK, Indonesia, Japan, the Republics of Mauritius and Seychelles, Suriname, Myanmar, and France. Because of a ten-year procedural clock that begins ticking when a country accedes to the convention, twenty-six additional states are expected to make their claims to the commission during the summer of 2009.

The urgency for the United States joining the convention is twofold. First, by not being a state party to the convention, the United States is unable to nominate or elect the expert commissioners who carry out the work of the CLCS. That reduces the ability of the United States to contribute to the work of the commission and ensure that the convention is applied fairly and objectively. Moreover, when Russia submitted what many considered an overly expansive claim in the Arctic Ocean in 2001, the U.S. ambassador to the UN, John Negroponte, could only file a demarche listing U.S. objections. By not acceding the convention, the United States has no standing before the commission in what will be the largest adjudication of state jurisdiction in world history.

Remaining a nonparty also prevents the United States from making its own submission to the commission. The State Department is currently overseeing an effort to collect evidence for an eventual American claim to the extended continental shelf, but the United States cannot formally submit this package for review by the CLCS until it formally joins the convention. By not joining, the United States is actually *giving up* sovereign rights—missing an opportunity for international recognition for a massive expansion of U.S. resources jurisdiction over as much as one million square kilometers of ocean, an area half the size of the Louisiana Purchase. Remaining outside the convention prevents the United States from participating in the process of overseeing the claims of other countries to the extended continental shelf and from formally making its own.

The second major economic issue that makes acceding to the convention urgent is the ongoing work of the International Seabed Authority, which oversees the minerals regime established by the convention for seabed areas outside national jurisdiction. The ISA's charter, as amended in the 1994 Agreement on Implementation, governs the international seabed based essentially on free market principles. By remaining a nonparty, the United States cannot fill its permanent seat on the ISA and is thus unable to exercise its special veto power over decisions on certain specified matters. U.S. deep-sea mining companies used to be among the world's most promising, but they have withered away without the legal protection that would come with the United States being a state party. American energy and deep-seabed companies have been put at a disadvantage in making investments for seabed minerals projects by the legal uncertainty accompanying the United States remaining a nonparty. Furthermore, U.S. firms cannot obtain international recognition of mine sites or title to recovered minerals.

The vastness of ocean space and the limits of our knowledge concerning the oceans' future economic potential also make it critically important that the United States plays a central role in the future implementation of the convention. The convention facilitates the conduct of marine scientific research to expand understanding of the marine realm. As knowledge increases and as technology advances, the oceans may hold enormous, and as yet only dimly perceived, potential. When coupled with America's unrivaled capacity for technological innovation, new ocean uses may become essential to helping drive economic prosperity for future generations. In the midst of a historic economic crisis, the United States needs to position itself by joining the treaty in order to secure its share of ocean industries of the future and the high-paying jobs they will create.

ENVIRONMENTAL

Protection of the marine environment was a core U.S. objective during the Law of the Sea negotiations. The ecological challenges that preoccupied U.S. negotiating teams a generation ago, such as the conservation of marine mammals and fish, have only become more acute in the intervening years. One in three marine mammal species is now considered vulnerable to extinction,[19] and it is estimated that the oceans have lost more than 90 percent of their large predatory fish since the advent of industrial fishing.[20] The convention's living-resources articles create a framework for international cooperation in the sustainable management of fish stocks and the conservation of marine mammals. That framework has helped mitigate downward trends since becoming operational, and it offers the United States tools it could utilize for conservation ends if it participated in the Law of the Sea regime. The 1995 UN Fish Stocks Agreement offers a prime example of how a carefully constructed international accord negotiated within the framework of the convention can provide for a legal binding conservation regime. Recognizing the utility of this specific fisheries management tool, the United States rapidly ratified this additional instrument as soon as it was possible to do so in 1996.

The convention's provisions on environmental protection address all sources of marine pollution, from ships and waste disposal at sea, in coastal areas and estuaries, to airborne particles. They create a framework for further developing measures to prevent, reduce, and control pollution globally, regionally, and nationally, and they call for measures to protect and preserve rare or fragile ecosystems, the habitat of depleted, threatened, or endangered species, and other forms of marine life.

Those facts alone argue strongly for U.S. accession. To answer the question "Why now?" however, a daunting set of comparatively new ecological threats must be considered. Climate change and the burgeoning industrialization of the oceans are giving rise to severe environmental stresses that require an urgent global response. U.S. leadership is critical, not only in undertaking the research that will help us understand the effects of climate change in the marine environment and related mitigation and adaptation options, but also in tackling the problems head-on. In many respects, such leadership cannot be fully realized without accession to the convention.

Oceans are among the first casualties of increased greenhouse-gas emissions. In preindustrial times, the oceans released an amount of carbon that roughly equaled the quantity they absorbed. But with rising levels of atmospheric CO_2, the seas are being asked to absorb more carbon than ever before, a process that has already increased the acidity of ocean surface waters by approximately 30 percent.[21] It is projected that global surface pH will decrease by a further 40 percent to 120 percent by the end of the century,[22] at which point the amount of CO_2 in the ocean will exceed levels seen at any time in the last three hundred million years.

Acidification carries with it the potential to devastate ocean ecosystems.[23] It will deprive marine animals of access to the calcium carbonate many of them require, weakening the formation of calcium carbonate shells. Commercially fished species that will be directly affected include corals, mussels, oysters, lobsters, and crabs. More important, however, is the likely impact on many species of small planktonic plants and animals that are crucial to marine food webs. In short, acidification has the potential to transform ocean life, and its impact is already being felt by America's marine environment.

A related consequence of climate change is ocean warming. The absorption by the ocean of excess heat in the atmosphere elevated ocean temperatures in the upper 700 meters by 0.1 degree Celsius between 1961 and 2003.[24] That ostensibly small temperature rise over such a vast expanse of water is, in fact, potentially devastating not only to ocean life but to life in general, because of the role ocean temperature plays in driving the planet's climate. The oceans store huge amounts of heat and distribute it across the globe. Even small changes in ocean temperature will have consequences for how that process occurs. As the oceans continue to warm, both the frequency and the intensity of hurricanes are predicted to increase. Scientists also predict more extreme maximum temperatures and more frequent heavy precipitation.[25]

Change is happening most rapidly, and can be seen most vividly, in the Arctic. The Arctic Ocean is the least understood of all the world's oceans, but we know it is warming at approximately twice the rate of the rest of the oceans. That is causing the rapid retreat of Arctic sea ice. In September 2007, the minimum ice extent at the end of summer was 23 percent lower than what it had been in 2005, the previous record low, and 50 percent lower than was typical in the 1950s through the 1970s.[26] Scientists from the National Snow and Ice Data Center and the National Center for Atmospheric Research have found that Arctic sea ice is melting even faster than models have projected, giving rise to predictions that the Arctic might be seasonally ice free as soon as 2013, and possibly earlier.

Such rapid change will lead to the local loss—or, in some cases, complete extinction—of certain Arctic species. Ice-associated marine algae and amphipods provide the base of the unique food web that includes a rich variety of invertebrates, fish, and birds. Ice-dependent ocean mammals, such as bowhead whales, narwhals, polar bears, ringed seals, and walruses, will also be directly affected by loss of habitat. The changes in the extent of Arctic sea ice will also have profound consequences for the world's climate, increasing the retention of solar heat and reducing the vital temperature gradient between the warmer tropics and colder polar regions, thus altering ocean currents and weather patterns throughout the Northern Hemisphere.

Attempts to mitigate climate change are the subject of separate international discussions. There is a strong argument to be made that acceding to the Law of the Sea Convention would strengthen America's diplomatic hand in those negotiations. Quite apart from that, however, the far-reaching changes to ocean ecosystems that are occurring as a result of climate change provide an answer to the question "Why now?" Full U.S. participation in the convention is vital as the international community adjusts to a rapidly changing ocean environment. The need to find ways to help humankind adapt to a changing climate will become increasingly important. Efforts to restore the natural resilience of marine ecosystems and species through their protection, maintenance, and restoration will be a central part of that effort. Given the geopolitical context of the Arctic region, U.S. leadership will be crucial.

The Arctic offers a particularly sobering environmental imperative. As its ecosystem comes under increasing strain from climate change, melting sea ice will expose it to unprecedented pressures that will accompany increased human access. Concerted international engagement to ensure effective and integrated ecosystem-based management of human activities in the Arctic is essential. Acceding to the convention would help the United States advance new governance initiatives in this important region, such as shipping-traffic schemes through the Bering Strait, coordinated sea route authorities, and possibly even the establishment of a marine scientific park at the North Pole. The convention provides solid legal bedrock on which to build elegant and effective governance structures for the future Arctic.

As the Law of the Sea regime becomes more entrenched, the international organs it has created are becoming more important policy-making centers. The continued absence of the United States from this international management regime deprives the United States of the opportunity to exercise environmental leadership over nearly three-quarters of the earth. Joining the convention would permit the United States to become the main force for responsible ocean stewardship at this critical juncture, rather than see the fate of the oceans determined by other players.

HOW REMAINING OUTSIDE THE CONVENTION DAMAGES U.S. NATIONAL INTERESTS

- The convention is now open for amendment and could be changed by countries hostile to U.S. interests if the United States does not participate in the process. The terms of the convention require accepting the treaty in toto, and joining now would allow the United States to lock in an agreement most favorable to its interests—and also gain the ability to apply maximum leverage against other states on strategic oceans issues. The longer it remains a nonparty, the more the United States cedes its negotiating strength.

- The convention provides two essential and immediate components for responding to piracy off the coast of Somalia. First, the convention permits any state to arrest pirates, seize pirate vessels, and prosecute pirates in the courts of the interdicting naval authority. Second, and equally important, the convention protects the sovereign rights of ocean-going states that participate in antipiracy naval operations in the territorial seas of failed states such as Somalia. This is critical for building international naval flotillas for combating the growing pirate problem in the Indian Ocean.

- The United States cannot currently participate in the Commission on the Limits of the Continental Shelf, which oversees ocean delineation on the outer limits of the extended continental shelf (outer continental shelf). Even though it is collecting scientific evidence to support eventual claims off its Atlantic, Gulf, and Alaskan coasts, the United States, without becoming party to the convention, has no standing in the CLCS. This not only precludes it from making a submission claiming the sovereign rights over the resources of potentially more than one million square kilometers of the OCS, it also denies the United States any right to review or contest other claims that appear to be overly expansive, such as Russia's in the Arctic. This is especially urgent this year, as the commission will review an influx of claims expected in May 2009, the deadline for twenty-six states to make their submissions based on the procedural clock that began ticking when they ratified the convention.

(The United States would have ten years to make its claim if it were to join the convention.)

- As evidenced by the controversy surrounding the March 2009 confrontation with the Chinese navy in the South China Sea, the United States today forfeits legal authority to other states, some of them less than friendly to U.S. interests, that seek to restrict rights enshrined in the Law of the Sea central to American national security strategy, such as the freedom of navigation. Other examples include proposals by the European Union for mandatory insurance certificates to enter European waters and Australia's pilotage requirements, both prejudicial to U.S. rights of innocent and transit passage.

- As long as it remains outside the convention, the United States is restricted from fully implementing the first-ever national Cooperative Strategy for 21st Century Seapower, jointly published by the chief of naval operations and the commandants of the Coast Guard and the Marine Corps, which seeks to build maritime partnerships for combating emerging threats based on the principles established in the convention. The United States also puts its sailors in unneeded jeopardy when carrying out the Freedom of Navigation program to contest Law of the Sea abuses.

- The United States cannot today expand the Proliferation Security Initiative with several critically important Pacific countries. Although supportive of U.S. counterproliferation efforts, these countries indicate that U.S. refusal to join the convention has eroded their confidence that the United States will abide by international law when conducting PSI interdiction activities.

- U.S. firms and citizens cannot take advantage of the arbitration processes established within the convention to defend their rights against foreign encroachment or abuse.

- The United States is unable to nominate a candidate for election to the Law of the Sea Tribunal and thus is deprived of the opportunity to directly shape the interpretation and application of the convention.

- The United States is in a weaker legal position in the opening of the Arctic to police new shipping, to contest disputed boundary claims, and to challenge Canada's assertion that the Northwest Passage falls within its internal waters.

– American energy and deep-seabed companies are at a disadvantage in making investments in the OCS due to the legal uncertainty over the outer limit of the U.S. continental shelf, nor can they obtain international recognition (and, as a result, financing) for mine sites or title to recovered minerals on the deep seabed beyond national jurisdiction. Even if U.S. firms were to unilaterally set out on their own, because the United States has negligible mineral-processing technology, they would have difficulty finding international partners to buy unprocessed minerals because they would have been obtained outside of the agreed regime.

– The United States is unable to fill its permanent seat on the Council of the International Seabed Authority and thus to influence this body's work overseeing minerals development in the deep seabed beyond national jurisdiction.

Conclusions and Recommendations

The arguments favoring the convention far outweigh those opposing it, and the United States should immediately join the 1982 Convention on the Law of the Sea. Of the treaties awaiting the Senate's advice and consent, this agreement is extraordinary in its implications for the national interest. As a result, the convention is getting a fresh look in Washington within the context of the current geopolitical seascape. The politics surrounding U.S. accession have also changed with a supportive president, secretary of state, and SFRC chair combined with the likelihood of more votes in the Senate. The convention is now poised to receive the Senate's advice and consent as required by the Constitution of the United States.

Driving the convention's reappraisal are the substantive issues demanding action. An increasingly assertive Chinese navy, a spike in pirate attacks in the Indian Ocean, and the opening of the Arctic to international shipping and resource extraction are but a few of the pressing issues that give mounting urgency for the United States to join the convention. Beyond these national security issues, and from an environmental perspective, the oceans realm is in deep distress in many parts of the world, and no nation acting alone can remedy this. Collaboration on the basis of the convention offers by far the sharpest arrow in the international community's quiver for responding, and by joining, the United States will gain a leadership role for responding to such environmental challenges.

In addition to the specific benefits to the national interest accrued from joining the convention, an internationally visible and successful bipartisan campaign that culminated in the United States joining the treaty this year could provide a springboard for a broader foreign policy agenda. Such a campaign would immediately

- Enhance U.S. global credibility by matching action to rhetoric regarding the rule of law. Joining this particular convention sends a powerful signal of commitment to this principle. The undeniable semantic message of the title "*Law* of the Sea" and the practical effect of officially becoming party to a legal regime over the vast expanse of the world's oceans combine to reinforce the strength of this signal.

- Convey broadly recognized legal legitimacy to U.S.-led security arrangements, such as PSI and its counterpiracy, -narcotic, and -terrorism operations at sea.

- Establish the foundation for strengthening existing international relationships and building new partnerships. By clearly signaling a U.S. commitment to respect the legitimate rights of other nations, while reinforcing an expectation of reciprocity, the United States can dispel suspicion and remove resistance in a global constituency.

- Provide an array of diplomatic tools to address "creeping sovereignty" and the excessive, resource-motivated claims of some coastal nations. Arbitration will allow the peaceful resolution of disputes with convention party states whether they are friends and partners, such as Canada, Australia, and the Philippines, or potential competitors, such as China. When diplomacy must be supplemented by hard power to challenge the excessive and disruptive claims of any nation, especially those of potential adversaries and nonparty states, such as Iran, Syria, and North Korea, the convention will provide the United States with legal legitimacy and at least the tacit support of 156 party states.

- Enable the United States to take a leadership position by acting within the convention to help mitigate maritime disputes between important strategic allies, such as Japan and Korea, and in strategically important regions, such as the Gulf of Aden or the South China Sea.

- Expand opportunity for U.S. global engagement and leadership by opening participation in the bodies and commissions established by the convention, especially the economically critical Commission on the Limits of the Continental Shelf and the International Seabed Authority, where the United States would become the only nation to gain a permanent seat and attendant influence.

- Strengthen U.S. leadership in combating maritime environmental challenges of increasing urgency, such as ocean acidification, collapsing fishing stocks, and pollution.

More difficult to measure than what would be gained from U.S. accession is the diplomatic blight on America's reputation for rejecting a carefully negotiated accord that enjoys overwhelming international consensus, one that has been adjusted specifically to meet the demands put forth by President Reagan two decades ago. Remaining outside the convention undermines U.S. credibility abroad and limits the ability of the United States to achieve its national security objectives. The treaty was negotiated over decades during which American delegations scored important victories. To the dismay of the rest of the world that negotiated the convention with the United States in good faith (and is now proceeding in making ocean policy and setting legal precedent in forums where U.S. influence is diminished), after fifteen years the Senate has yet to have an up or down vote.

The 1982 Convention on the Law of the Sea may seem an obscure agreement to nonexperts. That is not the case. The convention is a carefully negotiated international agreement numbering several hundred pages that covers a host of measurable national security, economic, and environmental issues of vital strategic importance to the United States. By remaining a nonparty to the convention, the United States not only forfeits these concrete interests but also undermines something more intangible: the legitimacy of U.S. leadership and its international reputation. For example, American pleas for other nations to follow pollution and fishing agreements ring empty when the United States visibly rejects the Law of the Sea Convention. Remaining outside the convention also hurts its diplomatic hand in other international forums, as well as the perceptions of other states about U.S. commitments to multilateral solutions. As former Supreme Court justice Sandra Day O'Connor has noted, "The decision not to sign on to legal frameworks the rest of the world supports is central to the decline of American influence around the world."[27]

Given the unprecedented challenges, threats, and opportunities the United States currently faces, it is as important as ever at this critical juncture to strengthen American influence and diplomatic leadership. Historically, one of the underlying foundations of U.S. global leadership has been a perceived commitment to the international rule of law and willingness to build international institutions that create a predictable international order from which all peace-loving countries can benefit. Acceding to the Law of the Sea Convention will help undergird continued U.S. leadership, by sending a tangible signal that the United States remains committed to its historic role as an architect and defender of world order.

From this perspective, acceding to the convention is low-hanging fruit to advance a much broader U.S. foreign policy agenda. It has the broadest bipartisan domestic support; supplies the most direct national security, economic, and environmental benefits for the United States; and has genuine global reach.

A committed political effort to join the convention during 2009 will provide a highly visible demonstration to a world audience that U.S. leadership has the resolve to match words with actions, especially when domestic follow-through means expending political capital. Breaking the fifteen-year stalemate in the Senate on the convention will be a strong signal that the United States is committed to multilateral agreements, especially those whose development both Republican and Democrat presidents and a strong bipartisan caucus in Congress champion. Therefore:

1. The central and strongest recommendation of this report is that the Senate should exercise its constitutional authority by offering its consent for the United States to formally join the 1982 Convention on the Law of the Sea.

2. In doing so, the Senate should consider the carefully worded and painstakingly crafted text resolution of advice and consent submitted as part of the SFRC Executive Report in December 2007 (Appendix III). This draft resolution chooses arbitration for dispute settlement and makes other important declarations, understandings, and interpretations that safeguard U.S. interests. These details are not insignificant, specifying U.S. exemption from mandatory dispute settlement in certain cases; requiring legislation for implementation in U.S. waters and to guide interpretation in U.S. courts; and preserving Senate oversight over any future amendments to the convention. If the Senate takes the convention up again this year, it would also have another opportunity to revisit this text of advice and consent and could make additional declarations, interpretations, and understandings needed to safeguard U.S. sovereignty.

3. For the reasons listed in this report, the president should consider making U.S. accession to the convention a leading foreign policy initiative in 2009.

Why is it imperative for the United States to join the convention?
Why now? To fail to join the convention this year would be to lose a
unique opportunity. The United States is experiencing a conjunction
of circumstances that includes the "fresh start" effect of a new administration, the ascendance of two national security strategies founded
on conflict prevention and partnership building, and a community of
nations eager for renewed American multilateralism. By joining the
convention now, the United States gains legal protection; for its sovereignty; sovereign rights and jurisdiction in offshore zones, the freedom of maneuver and action for its military forces; and protection for
economic, environmental, and marine research interests at sea while
seizing an opportunity to restore the mantle of international leadership on, over, and under nearly three-quarters of the earth. It is a bipartisan agenda, and one in the strategic interests of the United States. The
Senate should proceed this year and offer its advice and consent of the
Law of the Sea Convention.

Appendix I

REVIEW OF CRITICAL CONCERNS[28]

The decision to enter a significant international agreement demands a thorough and deliberative review that appropriately generates a number of critical concerns. This section reviews the concerns most often raised about the convention and the rationale of the associated majority and minority opinions.

Nearly twenty years of negotiation and renegotiation, the incorporation of substantive changes by the addition of agreements, and an execution mechanism under U.S. law that applies a resolution of advice and consent make understanding the legal implications of joining the convention a challenge, even for dedicated scholars. The fact that a well-respected president opposed the convention citing "several major problems in the Convention's deep seabed mining provisions"[29] that would endanger U.S. interests has led a minority of public opinion leaders to persistently oppose accession. After these problems were addressed by the 1994 agreement and the convention was submitted to the Senate by two later presidents, some opinion leaders continue to cite concerns that the convention poses risk to U.S. national interests.

In its 1982 form, the convention contained "unacceptable elements"[30] that led President Reagan to declare:

> "We have now completed a review of that convention and recognize that it contains many positive and very significant accomplishments. Those extensive parts dealing with navigation and overflight and most other provisions of the convention are consistent with United States interests and, in our view, serve well the interests of all nations. That is an important achievement and signifies the benefits of working together and effectively balancing numerous interests. . . . Our review recognizes, however, that the deep seabed mining part of the convention does not meet United States objectives. For this reason, I am announcing today that the United States will not sign the convention . . ."[31]

The outcome of U.S. action to legally remedy the unacceptable elements, after the convention was adopted by the General Assembly for ratification, was a complex body of related documents. To completely comprehend the implication of U.S. accession in 2009 requires an appreciation of customary treaty language combined with an understanding of the integrated effects of the original 1982 instrument, the 1994 agreement relating to the implementation of Part XI, and the proposed Senate Resolution of Advice and Consent.

CONCERNS RELATED TO NATIONAL SECURITY

As developed in earlier sections of this report, the majority opinion holds that joining the convention will enhance national security. The most prevalent minority opinions cite concerns regarding detrimental effects on:

– **Military Operations.** U.S. military forces are already legally bound to follow the provisions of convention by virtue of President Reagan's 1983 Statement on Ocean Policy; therefore, joining the convention will impose no additional restrictions on U.S. military operations. Since the completion of the 1994 agreement, there has been unanimous support for joining the convention by uniformed and civilian national security leaders, including the chairman and Joint Chiefs of Staff, the combatant commanders, and the commandant of the Coast Guard. The public record documenting historical and current support by national security leaders is overwhelming.[32] The most recent testimony of Deputy Secretary of Defense Gordon England succinctly captures this support:

> "President Bush, Secretary Gates, the Joint Chiefs of Staff, the Military Department Secretaries, the Combatant Commanders, the Commandant of the Coast Guard and I urge the Committee to give its approval for U.S. accession to the Law of the Sea Convention and ratification of the 1994 Agreement. The United States needs to join the Law of the Sea Convention, and join it now, to take full advantage of the many benefits it offers, to mitigate the increasing costs of being on the outside, and to support the global mobility of our armed forces and the sustainment of our combat forces overseas."[33]

– **Intelligence Operations.** State and Defense Department officials referencing closed hearings indicate that the executive branch, responsible for collecting and the principle consumer of classified intelligence, has no concerns that joining the convention will harm intelligence operations: "The Convention does not prohibit or impair intelligence or submarine activities. Joining the Convention would not affect the conduct of intelligence activities in any way. . . . Our intelligence activities will not be hampered by the Convention."[34]

– **The Proliferation Security Initiative.** Similar to concerns related to intelligence activities, the effect of convention accession on the PSI is best addressed by those executive branch departments responsible for its creation and execution. Ambassador John R. Bolton, undersecretary of state for arms control and international security affairs during the creation of the PSI, has stated: "I don't think that if the Senate were to ratify the Law of the Sea Treaty and the president were to make the treaty, that it would have any negative impact whatsoever on PSI." [35]

   The vice chief of naval operations has provided testimony that indicates joining the convention is necessary for, not harmful to, further PSI success: "[O]ur failure to be a Party to the Law of the Sea Convention is limiting further expansion of PSI. Critically important democratic Pacific countries have indicated a desire to support our counter-proliferation efforts, but they tell us that so long as we are not a Party to the Law of the Sea Convention, they will not be able . . . to endorse PSI."[36]

– **U.S. Technological Advantage.** It is true that the 1982 form of the convention mandated private technology transfer detrimental to U.S. national security and economic interests. That was one of the factors specifically cited when President Reagan rejected the convention. Article 144 of the convention does encourage technology transfer, calls for parties to "cooperate in promoting the transfer of technology and scientific knowledge," and remains in force following the adoption of the 1994 agreement but does not mandate technology transfer. Such transfer, mandated by Annex III Article 5 of the convention, was eliminated by section 5 of the annex to the 1994 agreement. Additional protection against national security damage through technology transfer is provided by Article 302 of the convention: "[N]othing in this Convention shall be deemed to require a State Party, in the fulfillment of its obligations under this Convention, to supply information the disclosure of which is contrary to the essential interests of its security."

A less prevalent but important minority opinion related to national security holds that the convention was developed with the participation of national liberation movements and these movements are allowed to participate as observers in the International Seabed Authority. Additionally, provisions of the convention that allow the distribution of ISA revenue to "peoples who have not attained full independence or other self-governing status" could be used to fund national liberation movements. President Reagan cited such provisions as a specific reason for rejecting the convention, since they allowed the possibility of channeling funds to groups the United States identified as terrorist organizations. While it is true that Article 156 of the convention allowed national liberation movements to sign the Final Act of the Third Conference on the Law of Sea and to participate as observers at the ISA, this observer status conveys no authority or voting rights and is equivalent to the status such movements are already granted in the UN General Assembly. It is also true that the ISA could possibly decide to distribute economic benefits to such movements if revenue becomes available in the future. The U.S. safeguard against such transfers becomes operative through the interaction of the convention and the 1994 agreement. Convention Article 161, paragraph 8(d) requires consensus of the ISA council to distribute economic benefits, pursuant to Article 162. Section 3, paragraph 15(a) of the annex to the 1994 agreement provides the United States a permanent seat on the council by virtue of being the largest economy on the date of entry into force of the convention. Together these sections effectively give the United States a "permanent veto" over distribution of economic benefits, hence preventing funds from being channeled to potential terrorist groups or other organizations likely to act counter to U.S. national security interests. Notably, the United States is the only nation with access to such a "permanent veto," which is only available upon joining the convention. Accordingly, President Reagan's concern regarding potential distribution of funds contrary to national security interests remains valid until the United States joins the convention.

CONCERNS RELATED TO NATIONAL SOVEREIGNTY

The majority opinion holds that the convention extends the sovereignty of coastal nations in a manner that significantly benefits the United States. Some minority opinion leaders have expressed concerns that joining the convention will erode U.S. sovereignty by observing that:

– **Amendments to the convention may become binding on the United States without the advice and consent of the Senate.**

   Article 316 of the convention has always required that most amendments be specifically ratified by a state before binding that state. The only exceptions to this requirement are for amendments to the Statute of the International Tribunal of the Law of the Sea, Annex VI, and for amendments relating to provisions on seabed mining. Amendments to Annex VI can only be adopted "without objection" per Article 313 or by consensus. In either case, the United States can block passage if necessary to obtain the advice and consent of the Senate. President Reagan's specific objection regarding amendments to seabed-mining provisions was remedied by the interaction of the 1994 agreement and the convention. Convention Article 161, paragraph 8(d) requires consensus of the ISA council to adopt amendments to Part XI, which contains the seabed-mining provisions. Section 3, paragraph 15(a) of the annex to the 1994 agreement provides the United States a permanent seat on the council by virtue of being the largest economy on the date of entry into force of the convention. Together these sections effectively give the United States a "permanent veto" over binding amendments to the seabed provisions of the convention. Similar to concerns regarding distribution of benefits to national liberation movements, the United States must join the convention and claim a seat on the ISA to enjoy these protections against unfavorable amendments. Failure to join the convention and participate in the ISA risks "poisoning" the convention to U.S. accession by the addition of unacceptable amendments.

– **Seabed resources beyond the limits of national jurisdiction are designated as the "common heritage of mankind."**

   This language does appear in the convention and was not affected by the 1994 agreement. The convention uses this designation to establish a defined legal regime that will protect deep-seabed investment by providing internationally enforceable property rights. To administer these rights, the ISA is empowered to levy application fees, review and act on claims, and then collect royalties from seabed exploitation operations. This process mirrors that used by countries around the world to promote exploitation of resources within the EEZ. The International Tribunal for the Law of the Sea is empowered to resolve some disputes related to Part XI of the convention in its Seabed Disputes Chamber. While these provisions of the convention are undeniable, they do not aggregate to a loss of sovereignty since the United States exercises no sovereign rights over seabed resources beyond the limits of national jurisdiction. These provisions provide a mechanism for private interests to acquire long-term, commercially exploitable rights that could not be guaranteed under U.S. law alone. Upon joining the convention the United States will not gain control over deep-seabed resources but will gain unique and significant influence as the only nation guaranteed a permanent seat on the Council of the ISA.

– **Dispute resolution mechanisms of the convention are binding on the United States.**

This assertion is undeniable. The United States will, by declaration as detailed in the draft Senate Resolution of Advice and Consent, choose arbitration or special arbitration as the method applicable for most categories of disputes. That is consistent with many other international agreements, including the 1995 Agreement for the Implementation of Provisions of the Law of the Sea for the Conservation of Fish Stocks, which the United States joined in 1996. The use of such mechanisms is not considered a surrender of sovereignty by the majority. Some disputes specific to the resources of the seabed beyond national jurisdiction will be subject to resolution in the Seabed Disputes Chamber of the International Tribunal on the Law of the Sea. The jurisdiction of this chamber, by definition, falls outside areas of sovereign control. Finally, by declaration as detailed in the draft Senate Resolution of Advice and Consent, the United States will not accept any mandatory resolution mechanism for disputes concerning military activities, including military activities by government vessels and aircraft engaged in noncommercial service. The sovereign immunity of U.S. vessels and aircraft on government service will be protected by the convention.

– Convention provisions that require action to control pollution may be used to force U.S. compliance with international agreements the Senate has not ratified.

It is true that Articles 194 and Part XV, section 5 require states to take "all measures consistent with this Convention that are necessary to prevent, reduce and control pollution of the marine environment from any source" and "adopt laws and regulations to prevent, reduce and control pollution of the marine environment from" the land and atmosphere under their jurisdiction. Convention provisions also call for states to reduce pollution by "the best practicable means at their disposal and in accordance with their capabilities" and to "endeavor to establish global and regional rules" to prevent and control pollution. The majority opinion holds that these provisions of the convention only bind the United States to act in accordance with its own laws or appropriately ratified international agreements and cannot be used as a "back door" to compel enforcement of international agreements the Senate has not ratified.

Appendix II

The White House, October 7, 1994

To the Senate of the United States:

I transmit herewith, for the advice and consent of the Senate to accession, the United Nations Convention on the Law of the Sea, with Annexes, done at Montego Bay, December 10, 1982 (the "Convention"), and, for the advice and consent of the Senate to ratification, the Agreement Relating to the Implementation of Part XI of the United Nations Convention on the Law of the Sea of 10 December 1982, with Annex, adopted at New York, July 28, 1994 (the "Agreement"), and signed by the United States, subject to ratification, on July 29, 1994. Also transmitted for the information of the Senate is the report of the Department of State with respect to the Convention and Agreement, as well as Resolution II of Annex I and Annex II of the Final Act of the Third United Nations Conference on the Law of the Sea.

The United States has basic and enduring national interests in the ocean and has consistently taken the view that the full range of these interests is best protected through a widely accepted international framework governing uses of the sea. Since the late 1960s, the basic U.S. strategy has been to conclude a comprehensive treaty on the law of the sea that will be respected by all countries. Each succeeding U.S. Administration has recognized this as the cornerstone of U.S. oceans policy. Following adoption of the Convention in 1982, it has been the policy of the United States to act in a manner consistent with its provisions relating to traditional uses of the oceans and to encourage other countries to do likewise.

The primary benefits of the Convention to the United States include the following:

– The Convention advances the interests of the United States as a global maritime power. It preserves the right of the U.S. military to use the world's oceans to meet national security requirements and of commercial vessels to carry sea-going cargoes. It achieves this, *inter alia*, by stabilizing the breadth of the territorial sea at 12 nautical miles; by setting forth navigation regimes of innocent passage in the territorial sea, transit passage in straits used for international navigation, and archipelagic sea lanes passage; and by reaffirming the traditional freedoms of navigation and overflight in the exclusive economic zone and the high seas beyond.

– The Convention advances the interests of the United States as a coastal state. It achieves this, *inter alia*, by providing for an exclusive economic zone out to 200 nautical miles from shore and by securing our rights regarding resources and artificial islands, installations and structures for economic purposes over the full extent of the continental shelf. These provisions fully comport with U.S. oil and gas leasing practices, domestic management of coastal fishery resources, and international fisheries agreements.

– As a far-reaching environmental accord addressing vessel source pollution, pollution from seabed activities, ocean dumping, and land-based sources of marine pollution, the Convention promotes continuing improvement in the health of the world's oceans.

– In light of the essential role of marine scientific research in the understanding and managing of the oceans, the Convention sets forth criteria and procedures to promote access to marine areas, including coastal waters, for research activities.

– The Convention facilitates solutions to the increasingly complex problems of the uses of the ocean—solutions that respect the essential balance between our interests as both a coastal and a maritime nation.

– Through its dispute settlement provisions, the Convention provides for mechanisms to enhance compliance by Parties with the Convention's provisions.

Notwithstanding these beneficial provisions of the Convention and bipartisan support for them, the United States decided not to sign the Convention in 1982 because of flaws in the regime it would have established for managing the development of mineral resources of the seabed beyond national jurisdiction (Part XI). It has been the consistent view of successive U.S. Administrations that this deep seabed mining regime was inadequate and in need of reform if the United States was ever to become a Party to the Convention.

Such reform has now been achieved. The Agreement, signed by the United States on July 29, 1994, fundamentally changes the deep seabed mining regime of the Convention. As described in the report of the Secretary of State, the Agreement meets the objections the United States and other industrialized nations previously expressed to Part XI. It promises to provide a stable and internationally recognized framework for mining to proceed in response to future demand for minerals.

Early adherence by the United States to the Convention and the Agreement is important to maintain a stable legal regime for all uses of the sea, which covers more than 70 percent of the surface of the globe. Maintenance of such stability is vital to U.S. national security and economic strength.

I therefore recommend that the Senate give early and favorable consideration to the Convention and to the Agreement and give its advice and consent to accession to the Convention and to ratification of the Agreement. Should the Senate give such advice and consent, I intend to exercise the options concerning dispute settlement recommended in the accompanying report of the Secretary of State.

WILLIAM J. CLINTON

STATEMENT BY THE PRESIDENT

THE WHITE HOUSE

Office of the Press Secretary

For Immediate Release
May 15, 2007

I am acting to advance U.S. interests in the world's oceans in two important ways.

First, I urge the Senate to act favorably on U.S. accession to the
United Nations Convention on the Law of the Sea during this session of Congress. Joining will serve the national security interests of
the United States, including the maritime mobility of our armed forces
worldwide. It will secure U.S. sovereign rights over extensive marine
areas, including the valuable natural resources they contain. Accession
will promote U.S. interests in the environmental health of the oceans.
And it will give the United States a seat at the table when the rights that
are vital to our interests are debated and interpreted.

Second, I have instructed the U.S. delegation to the International
Maritime Organization (IMO) to submit a proposal for international
measures that would enhance protection of the Papahanaumokuakea
Marine National Monument, the area including the Northwestern
Hawaiian Islands.

Last June, I issued a proclamation establishing the Monument, a
1,200-mile stretch of coral islands, seamounts, banks, and shoals that
are home to some 7,000 marine species. The United States will propose
that the IMO designate the entire area as a Particularly Sensitive Sea
Area (PSSA)—similar to areas such as the Florida Keys, the Great Bar-
rier Reef, and the Galapagos Archipelago—which will alert mariners to
exercise caution in the ecologically important, sensitive, and hazardous
area they are entering. This proposal, like the Convention on the Law
of the Sea, will help protect the maritime environment while preserving the navigational freedoms essential to the security and economy of
every nation.

Appendix III

*TEXT OF DRAFT RESOLUTION OF
ADVICE AND CONSENT TO RATIFICATION
SUBMITTED AS PART OF SFRC EXECUTIVE
REPORT 110-9*

Resolved (two-thirds of the Senators present concurring therein),

SECTION I. SENATE ADVICE AND CONSENT SUBJECT TO DECLARATIONS AND UNDERSTANDINGS.

The Senate advises and consents to the accession to the United Nations Convention on the Law of the Sea, with annexes, adopted on December 10, 1982 (hereafter in this resolution referred to as the "Convention"), and to the ratification of the Agreement Relating to the Implementation of Part XI of the United Nations Convention on the Law of the Sea, with annex, adopted on July 28, 1994 (hereafter in this resolution referred to as the "Agreement") (T.Doc. 103–39), subject to the declarations of section 2, to be made under articles 287 and 298 of the Convention, the declarations and understandings of section 3, to be made under article 310 of the Convention, and the conditions of section 4.

SECTION 2. DECLARATIONS UNDER ARTICLES 287 AND 298.

The advice and consent of the Senate under section 1 is subject to the following declarations:

(1) The Government of the United States of America declares, in accordance with article 287(1), that it chooses the following means for the settlement of disputes concerning the interpretation or application of the Convention:

> (A) a special arbitral tribunal constituted in accordance with Annex VIII for the settlement of disputes concerning the

interpretation or application of the articles of the Convention relating to (1) fisheries, (2) protection and preservation of the marine environment, (3) marine scientific research, and (4) navigation, including pollution from vessels and by dumping; and

(B) an arbitral tribunal constituted in accordance with Annex VII for the settlement of disputes not covered by the declaration in subparagraph (A).

(2) The Government of the United States of America declares, in accordance with article 298(1), that it does not accept any of the procedures provided for in section 2 of Part XV (including, inter alia, the Seabed Disputes Chamber procedure referred to in article 287(2)) with respect to the categories of disputes set forth in sub-paragraphs (a), (b), and (c) of article 298(1). The United States further declares that its consent to accession to the Convention is conditioned upon the understanding that, under article 298(1)(b), each State Party has the exclusive right to determine whether its activities are or were "military activities" and that such determinations are not subject to review.

SECTION 3. OTHER DECLARATIONS AND UNDERSTANDINGS UNDER ARTICLE 310.

The advice and consent of the Senate under section 1 is subject to the following declarations and understandings:

(1) The United States understands that nothing in the Convention, including any provisions referring to "peaceful uses" or "peaceful purposes," impairs the inherent right of individual or collective self-defense or rights during armed conflict.

(2) The United States understands, with respect to the right of innocent passage under the Convention, that—

(A) all ships, including warships, regardless of, for example, cargo, armament, means of propulsion, flag, origin, destination, or purpose, enjoy the right of innocent passage;

(B) article 19(2) contains an exhaustive list of activities that render passage non-innocent;

(C) any determination of non-innocence of passage by a ship must be made on the basis of acts it commits while in the territorial sea, and not on the basis of, for example, cargo, armament, means of propulsion, flag, origin, destination, or purpose; and

(D) the Convention does not authorize a coastal State to condition the exercise of the right of innocent passage by any ships, including warships, on the giving of prior notification to or the receipt of prior permission from the coastal State.

(3) The United States understands, concerning Parts III and IV of the Convention, that—

(A) all ships and aircraft, including warships and military aircraft, regardless of, for example, cargo, armament, means of propulsion, flag, origin, destination, or purpose, are entitled to transit passage and archipelagic sea lanes passage in their "normal mode";

(B) "normal mode" includes, inter alia—

(i) submerged transit of submarines;

(ii) overflight by military aircraft, including in military formation;

(iii) activities necessary for the security of surface warships, such as formation steaming and other force protection measures;

(iv) underway replenishment; and

(v) the launching and recovery of aircraft;

(C) the words "strait" and "straits" are not limited by geographic names or categories and include all waters not subject to Part IV that separate one part of the high seas or exclusive economic zone from another part of the high seas or exclusive economic zone or other areas referred to in article 45;

(D) the term "used for international navigation" includes all straits capable of being used for international navigation; and

(E) the right of archipelagic sea lanes passage is not dependent upon the designation by archipelagic States of specific sea lanes and/or air routes and, in the absence of such designation or if there has been only a partial designation, may be exercised through all routes normally used for international navigation.

(4) The United States understands, with respect to the exclusive economic zone, that—

(A) all States enjoy high seas freedoms of navigation and overflight and all other internationally lawful uses of the sea related to these freedoms, including, inter alia, military activities, such as anchoring, launching and landing of aircraft and other military devices, launching and recovering water-borne craft, operating military devices, intelligence collection, surveillance and reconnaissance activities, exercises, operations, and conducting military surveys; and

(B) coastal State actions pertaining to these freedoms and uses must be in accordance with the Convention.

(5) The United States understands that "marine scientific research" does not include, inter alia—

(A) prospecting and exploration of natural resources;

(B) hydrographic surveys;

(C) military activities, including military surveys;

(D) environmental monitoring and assessment pursuant to section 4 of Part XII; or

(E) activities related to submerged wrecks or objects of an archaeological and historical nature.

(6) The United States understands that any declaration or statement purporting to limit navigation, overflight, or other rights and freedoms of all States in ways not permitted by the Convention contravenes the Convention. Lack of a response by the United States to a particular declaration or statement made under the Convention shall not be interpreted as tacit acceptance by the United States of that declaration or statement.

(7) The United States understands that nothing in the Convention limits the ability of a State to prohibit or restrict imports of goods into its territory in order to, inter alia, promote or require compliance with environmental and conservation laws, norms, and objectives.

(8) The United States understands that articles 220, 228, and 230 apply only to pollution from vessels (as referred to in article 211) and not, for example, to pollution from dumping.

(9) The United States understands, with respect to articles 220 and 226, that the "clear grounds" requirement set forth in those articles is equivalent to the "reasonable suspicion" standard under United States law.

(10) The United States understands, with respect to article 228(2), that—

(A) the "proceedings" referred to in that paragraph are the same as those referred to in article 228(1), namely those proceedings in respect of any violation of applicable laws and regulations or international rules and standards relating to the prevention, reduction and control of pollution from vessels committed by a foreign vessel beyond the territorial sea of the State instituting proceedings; and

(B) fraudulent concealment from an officer of the United States of information concerning such pollution would extend the three-year period in which such proceedings may be instituted.

(11) The United States understands, with respect to article 230, that—

(A) it applies only to natural persons aboard the foreign vessels at the time of the act of pollution;

(B) the references to "monetary penalties only" exclude only imprisonment and corporal punishment;

(C) the requirement that an act of pollution be "willful" in order to impose non-monetary penalties would not constrain the imposition of such penalties for pollution caused by gross negligence;

(D) in determining what constitutes a "serious" act of pollution, a State may consider, as appropriate, the cumulative or aggregate impact on the marine environment of repeated acts of pollution over time; and

(E) among the factors relevant to the determination whether an act of pollution is "serious," a significant factor is non-compliance with a generally accepted international rule or standard.

(12) The United States understands that sections 6 and 7 of Part XII do not limit the authority of a State to impose penalties, monetary or non-monetary, for, inter alia—

(A) non-pollution offenses, such as false statements, obstruction of justice, and obstruction of government or judicial proceedings, wherever they occur; or

(B) any violation of national laws and regulations or applicable international rules and standards for the prevention, reduction and control of pollution of the marine environment that occurs while a foreign vessel is in any of its ports, rivers, harbors, or offshore terminals.

(13) The United States understands that the Convention recognizes and does not constrain the longstanding sovereign right of a State to impose and enforce conditions for the entry of foreign vessels into its ports, rivers, harbors, or offshore terminals, such as a requirement that ships exchange ballast water beyond 200 nautical miles from shore or a requirement that tank vessels carrying oil be constructed with double hulls.

(14) The United States understands, with respect to article 21(2), that measures applying to the "design, construction, equipment or manning" do not include, inter alia, measures such as traffic separation schemes, ship routing measures, speed limits, quantitative restrictions on discharge of substances, restrictions on the discharge and/or uptake of ballast water, reporting requirements, and record-keeping requirements.

(15) The United States understands that the Convention supports a coastal State's exercise of its domestic authority to regulate discharges into the marine environment resulting from industrial operations on board a foreign vessel.

(16) The United States understands that the Convention supports a coastal State's exercise of its domestic authority to regulate the introduction into the marine environment of alien or new species.

(17) The United States understands that, with respect to articles 61 and 62, a coastal State has the exclusive right to determine the allowable catch of the living resources in its exclusive economic zone, whether it has the capacity to harvest the entire allowable catch, whether any surplus exists for allocation to other States, and to establish the terms and conditions under which access may be granted. The United States further understands that such determinations are, by virtue of article 297(3)(a), not subject to binding dispute resolution under the Convention.

(18) The United States understands that article 65 of the Convention lent direct support to the establishment of the moratorium on commercial whaling, supports the creation of sanctuaries and other conservation measures, and requires States to cooperate not only with respect to large whales, but with respect to all cetaceans.

(19) The United States understands that, with respect to article 33, the term "sanitary laws and regulations" includes laws and regulations to protect human health from, inter alia, pathogens being introduced into the territorial sea.

(20) The United States understands that decisions of the Council pursuant to procedures other than those set forth in article 161(8)(d) will involve administrative, institutional, or procedural matters and will not result in substantive obligations on the United States.

(21) The United States understands that decisions of the Assembly under article 160(2)(e) to assess the contributions of members are to be taken pursuant to section 3(7) of the Annex to the Agreement and that the United States will, pursuant to section 9(3) of the Annex to the

Agreement, be guaranteed a seat on the Finance Committee established by section 9(1) of the Annex to the Agreement, so long as the Authority supports itself through assessed contributions.

(22) The United States declares, pursuant to article 39 of Annex VI, that decisions of the Seabed Disputes Chamber shall be enforceable in the territory of the United States only in accordance with procedures established by implementing legislation and that such decisions shall be subject to such legal and factual review as is constitutionally required and without precedential effect in any court of the United States.

(23) The United States—

(A) understands that article 161(8)(f) applies to the Council's approval of amendments to section 4 of Annex VI;

(B) declares that, under that article, it intends to accept only a procedure that requires consensus for the adoption of amendments to section 4 of Annex VI; and

(C) in the case of an amendment to section 4 of Annex VI that is adopted contrary to this understanding, that is, by a procedure other than consensus, will consider itself bound by such an amendment only if it subsequently ratifies such amendment pursuant to the advice and consent of the Senate.

(24) The United States declares that, with the exception of articles 177–183, article 13 of Annex IV, and article 10 of Annex VI, the provisions of the Convention and the Agreement, including amendments thereto and rules, regulations, and procedures thereunder, are not self-executing.

SECTION 4. CONDITIONS.

(a) IN GENERAL.—The advice and consent of the Senate under section 1 is subject to the following conditions:

(1) Not later than 15 days after the receipt by the Secretary of State of a written communication from the Secretary-General of the United Nations or the Secretary-General of the Authority transmitting a proposal to amend the Convention pursuant to article 312, 313, or 314, the President shall submit to the Committee on Foreign Relations of the Senate a copy of the proposed amendment.

(2) Prior to the convening of a Conference to consider amendments to the Convention proposed to be adopted pursuant to article 312 of the Convention, the President shall consult with the Committee on

Foreign Relations of the Senate on the amendments to be considered at the Conference. The President shall also consult with the Committee on Foreign Relations of the Senate on any amendment proposed to be adopted pursuant to article 313 of the Convention.

(3) Not later than 15 days prior to any meeting—

(A) of the Council of the International Seabed Authority to consider an amendment to the Convention proposed to be adopted pursuant to article 314 of the Convention; or

(B) of any other body under the Convention to consider an amendment that would enter into force pursuant to article 316(5) of the Convention; the President shall consult with the Committee on Foreign Relations of the Senate on the amendment and on whether the United States should object to its adoption.

(4) All amendments to the Convention, other than amendments under article 316(5) of a technical or administrative nature, shall be submitted by the President to the Senate for its advice and consent.

(5) The United States declares that it shall take all necessary steps under the Convention to ensure that amendments under article 316(5) are adopted in conformity with the treaty clause in Article II, section 2 of the United States Constitution.

(b) INCLUSION OF CERTAIN CONDITIONS IN INSTRUMENT OF RATIFICATION.—Conditions 4 and 5 shall be included in the States instrument of ratification to the Convention.

Endnotes

1. There is no official position about which articles of the convention the United States accepts as customary international law and which it rejects. Portions of the convention are identical to the 1958 conventions, to which the United States is a party and has treaty obligations. The closest public proclamation on the Law of the Sea is President Ronald Reagan's March 10, 1983, "Statement on U.S. Oceans Policy," in which he proclaimed the United States would accept the navigation and overflight articles but reject the deep-seabed mining provisions (which were later modified to address President Reagan's concerns in the 1994 agreement on implementation).

2. The SFRC first voted unanimously to approve the convention in 2003 and then in 2007 voted again in favor 17–4.

3. The convention was open for ratification for a two-year period following its adoption in 1982. Today, countries technically can only "accede" to the convention, not ratify it. The convention came into force on November 16, 1994, when sixty countries became state parties. The Agreement on Part XI, which was signed by the United States on July 29, 1994, entered into force on July 28, 1996. Now, since the convention has technically already been ratified, the United States will "accede" to, not ratify, the convention if the Senate offers its consent as required by the Constitution. If this were to happen, the United States will become a "state party" to the 1982 convention and the supplemental agreement of 1994.

4. In fact, the Law of the Sea might be the only issue on which the following individuals and constituencies all agree: presidents Clinton, George W. Bush, and Obama; every living chief of naval operations, Coast Guard commandant, and the Joint Chiefs of Staff; every living secretary of state and State Department legal adviser; the blue-ribbon U.S. Commission on Ocean Policy and the Pew Oceans Commission; major industry groups, including the Chamber of Commerce, the American Petroleum Institute, the Chamber of Shipping, the National Fisheries Institute, and the Undersea Cable Industry; leading environmental and conservation groups, including the World Wildlife Fund, the Ocean Conservancy, the International Union for Conservation of Nature, and the National Resources Defense Council; and major professional organizations, including the American Bar Association and the American Geophysical Union. The U.S. Commission on Ocean Policy, chaired by former energy secretary and CNO Admiral James D. Watkins (a member of this report's advisory committee), and the Pew Oceans Commission, chaired by current CIA director Leon Panetta, both strongly urged the United States to join the Law of the Sea. The Joint Ocean Commission Initiative, created when these two commissions merged, continues to actively work to advance the convention in the Senate.

5. U.S. Geological Survey Circum Arctic Resource Appraisal, released July 2008, http://energy.usgs.gov/arctic/.

6. Article 19, Law of the Sea Convention.

7. For the rest of the report "mile" is used interchangeably with "nautical mile," the unit of measure in the Law of the Sea. One nautical mile equals 1.15 statute miles.

8. Note verbale to Secretary-General U Thant, United Nations General Assembly Doc. A/6695, 22nd Session, August 18, 1967.

9. UN General Assembly Resolution 2749 (25th Session), December 17, 1970.

10. President Reagan's official "Statement on U.S. Oceans Policy," March 10, 1983, http://www.reagan.utexas.edu/archives/speeches/1983/31083d.htm.

11. Benjamin W. Labaree, et al., *America and the Sea* (Mystic, CT: Mystic Seaport, 1998).

12. Mark Kurlansky, *Cod—a Biography of the Fish that Changed the World* (New York: Walker & Co., 1997).

13. "Troubled Waters: A Special Report on the Sea," *The Economist*, January 3, 2009, p. 3.

14. Deborah Cramer, *Ocean—Our Water, Our World* (New York: HarperCollins, 2008), p. 271.

15. See Selig Adler, *The Isolationist Impulse: Its Twentieth-Century Reaction* (Westport, CT: Greenwood Press, 1974); Thomas N. Guinsburg, *The Pursuit of Isolationism in the United States Senate from Versailles to Pearl Harbor* (New York: Garland Pub., 1982); Manfred Jonas, *Isolationism in America, 1935–1941* (Ithaca, NY: Cornell University Press, 1966); Roland N. Stromberg, *Collective Security and American Foreign Policy—from the League of Nations to NATO* (New York: Praeger, 1963).

16. SFRC Report together with minority views, Executive Report 110-9, 110th Congress, 1st Session, December 19, 2007. The number of states parties has grown to 156 from 152 since 2007.

17. FCC International Bureau Report, February 2008, http://hraunfoss.fcc.gov/edocs_public/attachmatch/DOC-280335A1.pdf.

18. The strategy can be found at: http://www.navy.mil/maritime/MaritimeStrategy.pdf.

19. International Union for Conservation of Nature, 2008, *2008 IUCN Red List of Threatened Species.*

20. Ransom Myers and Boris Worm, "Rapid Worldwide Depletion of Predatory Fish Communities," *Nature*, May 15, 2003, vol. 423, pp. 280–83.

21. Intergovernmental Panel on Climate Change, 2007, *Fourth Assessment Report: Climate Change 2007.*

22. Ibid.

23. John M. Guinotte and Victoria J. Fabry, "Ocean Acidification and Its Potential Effects on Marine Ecosystems," *Annals of the New York Academy of Sciences*, 2008, vol. 1143, pp. 320–342.

24. IPCC, 2007.

25. Ibid.

26. National Snow and Ice Data Center, "Arctic Sea Ice Shatters All Previous Record Lows: Diminished Summer Sea Ice Leads to Opening of the Fabled Northwest Passage," http://nsidc.org/news/press/2007_seaiceminimum/20071001_pressrelease.html.

27. As communicated in a Center for Strategic and International Studies report on "smart power," http://www.csis.org/smartpower/.

28. With gratitude to Captain Brian Donegan, USN, who researched, vetted, and composed this appendix.

29. March 10, 1983, Presidential Statement, http://www.reagan.utexas.edu/archives/speeches/1983/31083d.htm.

30. January 29, 1982, Presidential Statement, http://www.reagan.utexas.edu/archives/speeches/1982/12982b.htm.

31. July 9, 1982, Presidential Statement, http://www.reagan.utexas.edu/archives/speeches/1982/70982b.htm.

32. Joint Chiefs of Staff Letter, http://www.virginia.edu/colp/pdf/Biden-Letter-JointChiefs.pdf; Vice Chief of Naval Operations SFRC testimony, September 27, 2007, http://www.virginia.edu/colp/pdf/WalshTestimony070927.pdf; Deputy Secretary of Defense SFRC testimony, September 27, 2007, http://www.virginia.edu/colp/pdf/EnglandTestimony070927.pdf.

33. Ibid.

34. Deputy Secretary of State SFRC testimony, September 27, 2007, http://www.virginia.edu/colp/pdf/NegroponteTestimony070927.pdf.

35. Undersecretary of State for Arms Control and International Security SFRC testimony, April 11, 2005.

36. Vice Chief of Naval Operations SFRC testimony, September 2007, http://www.virginia.edu/colp/pdf/WalshTestimony070927.pdf.

About the Author

Scott G. Borgerson is the visiting fellow for ocean governance at the Council on Foreign Relations (CFR). Before joining CFR, Dr. Borgerson was the director of the Institute for Leadership and an assistant professor at the U.S. Coast Guard Academy. During a decade on active duty, he also contributed to Coast Guard strategic planning efforts and served several tours at sea on narcotics interdiction and search and rescue missions, holding positions as navigator aboard the cutter *Dallas* and as commanding officer of the patrol boat *Point Sal*. Dr. Borgerson holds a U.S. Merchant Marine officer master's license, is a board member of the Institute for Global Maritime Studies, and is a principal of Rhumb Line LLC, an independent, maritime consulting firm. He earned a BS with high honors from the U.S. Coast Guard Academy as well as an MALD and a PhD in international relations, both from the Fletcher School of Law and Diplomacy at Tufts University.

Advisory Committee for
The National Interest and the Law of the Sea

Caitlyn Antrim
Oceanlaw.org

Randy Beardsworth
Catalyst Partners

Richard E. Bissell
National Academy of Sciences

Laura Cantral
Meridian Institute

Biliana Cicin-Sain
University of Delaware

Brian T. Donegan
Council on Foreign Relations

Stephen E. Flynn
Council on Foreign Relations

Alton Frye
Council on Foreign Relations

Sherri W. Goodman
CNA

James C. Greenwood
Biotechnology Industry Organization

Richard Herold
BP p.l.c.

Peter Hill
Consortium for Ocean Leadership

Theodore W. Kassinger
O'Melveny & Myers LLP

Lee Kimball
Independent

Michael A. Levi
Council on Foreign Relations

Oivind Lorentzen III
Northern Navigation America, Inc.

John Norton Moore
University of Virginia

Stewart M. Patrick
Council on Foreign Relations

Brian T. Petty
International Association of Drilling Contractors

Thomas R. Pickering
Hills & Company

James H. Power
Holland & Knight

David Rockefeller Jr.
Rockefeller & Co., Inc.

Wesley Scholz
U.S. Department of State

Vikki N. Spruill
Ocean Conservancy

John Temple Swing
Foreign Policy Association

James D. Watkins
Joint Ocean Commission Initiative

Timothy E. Wirth
United Nations Foundation

Note: Council Special Reports reflect the judgments and recommendations of the author(s). They do not necessarily represent the views of members of the advisory committee, whose involvement in no way should be interpreted as an endorsement of the report by either themselves or the organizations with which they are affiliated.

Mission Statement of the International Institutions and Global Governance Program

The International Institutions and Global Governance (IIGG) program at the Council on Foreign Relations (CFR) aims to identify the institutional requirements for effective multilateral cooperation in the twenty-first century. The program is motivated by recognition that the architecture of global governance—largely reflecting the world as it existed in 1945—has not kept pace with fundamental changes in the international system. These shifts include the spread of transnational challenges, the rise of new powers, and the mounting influence of nonstate actors. Existing multilateral arrangements thus provide an inadequate foundation for addressing many of today's most pressing threats and opportunities and for advancing U.S. national and broader global interests.

Given these trends, U.S. policymakers and other interested actors require rigorous, independent analysis of current structures of multilateral cooperation, and of the promises and pitfalls of alternative institutional arrangements. The IIGG program meets these needs by analyzing the strengths and weaknesses of existing multilateral institutions and proposing reforms tailored to new international circumstances.

The IIGG program fulfills its mandate by

- Engaging CFR fellows in research on improving existing and building new frameworks to address specific global challenges—including climate change, the proliferation of weapons of mass destruction, transnational terrorism, and global health—and disseminating the research through books, articles, Council Special Reports, and other outlets;

- Bringing together influential foreign policymakers, scholars, and CFR members to debate the merits of international regimes and frameworks at meetings in New York, Washington, DC, and other select cities;

- Hosting roundtable series whose objectives are to inform the foreign policy community of today's international governance challenges and breed inventive solutions to strengthen the world's multilateral bodies; and

- Providing a state-of-the-art Web presence as a resource to the wider foreign policy community on issues related to the future of global governance.

Council Special Reports

Published by the Council on Foreign Relations

Lessons of the Financial Crisis
Benn Steil; CSR No. 45, March 2009
A Maurice R. Greenberg Center for Geoeconomic Studies Report

Global Imbalances and the Financial Crisis
Steven Dunaway; CSR No. 44, March 2009
A Maurice R. Greenberg Center for Geoeconomic Studies Report

Eurasian Energy Security
Jeffrey Mankoff; CSR No. 43, February 2009

Preparing for Sudden Change in North Korea
Paul B. Stares and Joel S. Wit; CSR No. 42, January 2009
A Center for Preventive Action Report

Averting Crisis in Ukraine
Steven Pifer; CSR No. 41, January 2009
A Center for Preventive Action Report

Congo: Securing Peace, Sustaining Progress
Anthony W. Gambino; CSR No. 40, October 2008
A Center for Preventive Action Report

Deterring State Sponsorship of Nuclear Terrorism
Michael A. Levi; CSR No. 39, September 2008

China, Space Weapons, and U.S. Security
Bruce W. MacDonald; CSR No. 38, September 2008

Sovereign Wealth and Sovereign Power: The Strategic Consequences of American Indebtedness
Brad W. Setser; CSR No. 37, September 2008
A Maurice R. Greenberg Center for Geoeconomic Studies Report

Securing Pakistan's Tribal Belt
Daniel Markey; CSR No. 36, July 2008 (Web-only release) and August 2008
A Center for Preventive Action Report

Avoiding Transfers to Torture
Ashley S. Deeks; CSR No. 35, June 2008

Global FDI Policy: Correcting a Protectionist Drift
David M. Marchick and Matthew J. Slaughter; CSR No. 34, June 2008
A Maurice R. Greenberg Center for Geoeconomic Studies Report

Dealing with Damascus: Seeking a Greater Return on U.S.-Syria Relations
Mona Yacoubian and Scott Lasensky; CSR No. 33, June 2008
A Center for Preventive Action Report

Climate Change and National Security: An Agenda for Action
Joshua W. Busby; CSR No. 32, November 2007
A Maurice R. Greenberg Center for Geoeconomic Studies Report

Planning for Post-Mugabe Zimbabwe
Michelle D. Gavin; CSR No. 31, October 2007
A Center for Preventive Action Report

The Case for Wage Insurance
Robert J. LaLonde; CSR No. 30, September 2007
A Maurice R. Greenberg Center for Geoeconomic Studies Report

Reform of the International Monetary Fund
Peter B. Kenen; CSR No. 29, May 2007
A Maurice R. Greenberg Center for Geoeconomic Studies Report

Nuclear Energy: Balancing Benefits and Risks
Charles D. Ferguson; CSR No. 28, April 2007

Nigeria: Elections and Continuing Challenges
Robert I. Rotberg; CSR No. 27, April 2007
A Center for Preventive Action Report

The Economic Logic of Illegal Immigration
Gordon H. Hanson; CSR No. 26, April 2007
A Maurice R. Greenberg Center for Geoeconomic Studies Report

The United States and the WTO Dispute Settlement System
Robert Z. Lawrence; CSR No. 25, March 2007
A Maurice R. Greenberg Center for Geoeconomic Studies Report

Bolivia on the Brink
Eduardo A. Gamarra; CSR No. 24, February 2007
A Center for Preventive Action Report

After the Surge: The Case for U.S. Military Disengagement from Iraq
Steven N. Simon; CSR No. 23, February 2007

Darfur and Beyond: What Is Needed to Prevent Mass Atrocities
Lee Feinstein; CSR No. 22, January 2007

Avoiding Conflict in the Horn of Africa: U.S. Policy Toward Ethiopia and Eritrea
Terrence Lyons; CSR No. 21, December 2006
A Center for Preventive Action Report

Living with Hugo: U.S. Policy Toward Hugo Chávez's Venezuela
Richard Lapper; CSR No. 20, November 2006
A Center for Preventive Action Report

Reforming U.S. Patent Policy: Getting the Incentives Right
Keith E. Maskus; CSR No. 19, November 2006
A Maurice R. Greenberg Center for Geoeconomic Studies Report

Foreign Investment and National Security: Getting the Balance Right
Alan P. Larson, David M. Marchick; CSR No. 18, July 2006
A Maurice R. Greenberg Center for Geoeconomic Studies Report

Challenges for a Postelection Mexico: Issues for U.S. Policy
Pamela K. Starr; CSR No. 17, June 2006 (Web-only release) and November 2006

U.S.-India Nuclear Cooperation: A Strategy for Moving Forward
Michael A. Levi and Charles D. Ferguson; CSR No. 16, June 2006

Generating Momentum for a New Era in U.S.-Turkey Relations
Steven A. Cook and Elizabeth Sherwood-Randall; CSR No. 15, June 2006

Peace in Papua: Widening a Window of Opportunity
Blair A. King; CSR No. 14, March 2006
A Center for Preventive Action Report

Neglected Defense: Mobilizing the Private Sector to Support Homeland Security
Stephen E. Flynn and Daniel B. Prieto; CSR No. 13, March 2006

Afghanistan's Uncertain Transition From Turmoil to Normalcy
Barnett R. Rubin; CSR No. 12, March 2006
A Center for Preventive Action Report

Preventing Catastrophic Nuclear Terrorism
Charles D. Ferguson; CSR No. 11, March 2006

Getting Serious About the Twin Deficits
Menzie D. Chinn; CSR No. 10, September 2005
A Maurice R. Greenberg Center for Geoeconomic Studies Report

Both Sides of the Aisle: A Call for Bipartisan Foreign Policy
Nancy E. Roman; CSR No. 9, September 2005

Forgotten Intervention? What the United States Needs to Do in the Western Balkans
Amelia Branczik and William L. Nash; CSR No. 8, June 2005
A Center for Preventive Action Report

A New Beginning: Strategies for a More Fruitful Dialogue with the Muslim World
Craig Charney and Nicole Yakatan; CSR No. 7, May 2005

Power-Sharing in Iraq
David L. Phillips; CSR No. 6, April 2005
A Center for Preventive Action Report

Giving Meaning to "Never Again": Seeking an Effective Response to the Crisis in Darfur and Beyond
Cheryl O. Igiri and Princeton N. Lyman; CSR No. 5, September 2004

Freedom, Prosperity, and Security: The G8 Partnership with Africa: Sea Island 2004 and Beyond
J. Brian Atwood, Robert S. Browne, and Princeton N. Lyman; CSR No. 4, May 2004

Addressing the HIV/AIDS Pandemic: A U.S. Global AIDS Strategy for the Long Term
Daniel M. Fox and Princeton N. Lyman; CSR No. 3, May 2004
Cosponsored with the Milbank Memorial Fund

Challenges for a Post-Election Philippines
Catharin E. Dalpino; CSR No. 2, May 2004
A Center for Preventive Action Report

Stability, Security, and Sovereignty in the Republic of Georgia
David L. Phillips; CSR No. 1, January 2004
A Center for Preventive Action Report

To purchase a printed copy, call the Brookings Institution Press: 800.537.5487.
Note: Council Special Reports are available for download from CFR's website, www.cfr.org.
For more information, email publications@cfr.org.